Dawn Baker is a chartered psychologist and trained therapist in cognitive behavioral therapy (CBT). She has worked at the Depersonalisation Research Unit at the Institute of Psychiatry, King's College London, developing a psychological model of depersonalization disorder as well as treatment and management strategies. She also works as a clinical health psychologist for a mental health trust in central London.

Elaine Hunter is a trained psychologist and CBT therapist and has worked at the Depersonalisation Research Unit where she developed a CBT model of depersonalization disorder. Prior to this she carried out research into the psychological effects of abuse. She has since trained as a clinical psychologist and currently works in the South London and Maudsley NHS Foundation Trust and continues to research depersonalization disorder.

Emma Lawrence is an experimental psychologist working at the Institute of Psychiatry and Associate Lecturer for the Open University's cognitive psychology module. She was a runner-up in the 2002 *New Scientist* essay competition, and has twice been awarded the Public Engagement with Psychology grant by the British Psychological Society.

Anthony David was appointed Consultant Psychiatrist at the South London and Maudsley NHS Foundation Trust and Senior Lecturer in Psychiatry at the Institute of Psychiatry in 1990. He was awarded personal chair of the Institute in 1996 and was, until recently, Chairman of the British Neuropsychiatry Association. In 1998 he set up the first clinic for depersonalization disorder in the UK (the Depersonalisation Research Unit).

Contributing authors **Nick Medford** and **Mauricio Sierra** are both clinical psychiatrists working at the Depersonalisation Research Unit at the Institute of Psychiatry. Dr Sierra originally qualified in Colombia and did his PhD on depersonalization at Cambridge University. Dr Medford worked in neurology before
South London and Maudsley NHS F

The aim of the **Overcoming** series is to enable people with a range of
common problems and disorders to take control of their own recovery program.
Each title, with its specially tailored program, is devised by a practising
clinician using the latest techniques of cognitive behavioral therapy –
techniques which have been shown to be highly effective in changing the
way patients think about themselves and their problems.
The series was initiated in 1993 by Peter Cooper, Professor of Psychology
at Reading University in the UK, whose original book on overcoming
bulimia nervosa and binge-eating continues to help many people in the UK,
the USA, Australasia and Europe. Many books in the **Overcoming** series are recommended by
the UK Department of Health under the Books on Prescription scheme.

Other titles in the series include:

All titles in the series are available by mail order.
Please see the order form at the back of this book.
www.overcoming.co.uk

OVERCOMING DEPERSONALIZATION AND FEELINGS OF UNREALITY

A self-help guide using
Cognitive Behavioral Techniques

DAWN BAKER,
ELAINE HUNTER,
EMMA LAWRENCE
and
ANTHONY DAVID

ROBINSON

ROBINSON

First published in Great Britain by Robinson in 2007.
This edition published in 2010

Important Note
This book is not intended as a substitute for medical advice or treatment.
Any person with a condition requiring medical attention should consult
a qualified medical practitioner or suitable therapist.

A CIP catalogue record for this book
is available from the British Library.

ISBN 978-1-84529-554-7 (paperback)
ISBN 978-1-4721-0574-5 (ebook)

Printed and bound in Great Britain by Clys Ltd., St Ives plc

Robinson
is an imprint of
Constable & Robinson Ltd
100 Victoria Embankment
London EC4Y 0DY

An Hachette UK Company
www.hachette.co.uk

www.constablerobinson.com

3 5 7 9 10 8 6 4

Table of contents

Acknowledgments

The Depersonalisation Research Unit at the Institute of Psychiatry and Maudsley Hospital, London, opened in 1998 and was the first unit in the UK to specialize in depersonalization and feelings of unreality (DPAFU). The Unit was in part set up by a grant from the Pilkington family charities, to whom we are hugely indebted. The Pilkington family have shown enduring faith in our work and have continued to challenge us to improve our understanding of the condition and, hopefully, help to overcome it. The launch of the Unit was marked by an article in *The Times* by Dr Thomas Stuttaford (12 March 1998), which prompted a flood of enquiries from people seeking more information and help. The Unit was initially co-directed by psychiatrist Mary Phillips, whose work on emotion and the brain helped increase our appreciation of DPAFU and what might cause it. Many other individuals have contributed to the clinic over the years as psychologists and psychiatrists including Carl Senior PhD, Poppy Schoenberg, Dr Michele Lambert, Dr Maxine Patel and numerous visitors from abroad. In addition, work in the US by Dr Daphne Simeon's group has added to our knowledge about this condition and has therefore been drawn on throughout the book. The research undertaken in our Unit has also been supported by various additional funding agencies such as the Medical Research Council and Wellcome Trust. Most importantly, however, we would like to thank the people who experience DPAFU and who have agreed to take part in the numerous research studies our Unit has conducted. The Unit continues today as part of a national service within the South London and Maudsley National Health Service Foundation Trust. Referrals must come through a general practitioner or psychiatrist.

We also have some very personal acknowledgments we wish to make:

Dawn
For my children, Jodie, Leah, Alex, Isabelle and Hannah, and my god son Charlie. Not least Tony.

Elaine
To Prakash Bijwe for his love and wisdom.

Emma
To the three Ss, Julie, Caroline and all those who have supported me along the way.

Preface

This book has been produced by the Depersonalisation Research Unit at the Institute of Psychiatry and Maudsley Hospital, London. The Unit conducts various research projects as well as providing a clinical service to people who suffer with depersonalization/derealization disorder and feelings of unreality (DPAFU).

The book will help you to understand and manage your DPAFU using highly effective Cognitive Behavioral Therapy (CBT) strategies. Numerous research studies have shown that CBT works extremely well with a variety of different types of people and problems. In some people with DPAFU these strategies may help the problems all but disappear. With others the severity of the problems may reduce to the extent that the person can get on with their life again. In other cases the frequency of the DPAFU may lessen. You are likely to feel more in control of your problems and better able to cope. There may be a range of benefits derived from the techniques we suggest here. We can't promise this book will provide you with a complete cure since there may be factors beyond the scope of this book that need to be addressed, but you will learn strategies that are likely to have a positive impact on helping you feel better.

Using principles derived from CBT does not mean that the physical and biochemical aspects of DPAFU are not important – because they almost certainly are. In fact we believe that it is these very aspects that make depersonalization different from anxiety and depression. We will discuss these physical and biochemical aspects, along with medical (i.e. drug) and other treatments for depersonalization disorder. And though we believe the strategies we outline are likely to be of real benefit, this book isn't intended to be a replacement for treatment or therapy. If you feel you need to talk to a professional about your problems, then your GP may be able to help. If he or she can't help, a referral to a psychologist or psychiatrist may be appropriate.

The CBT approach helps people to look at the connections between how they *think*, how they *feel* and how they *behave*. The theory suggests that if the ideas, beliefs and values you hold are unrealistic or have become distorted, then 'negative' thinking patterns are likely to occur. Negative thinking patterns can lead to negative feelings such as loss of confidence, feeling low and anxiety. When you feel low or anxious you often change your behavior. For instance, you may feel less like socializing, and so you go out less. If you go out less you may end up feeling lonely, which in turn leads to a lower mood. This can develop into a downward spiral that feels as if it is difficult to break on your own. This cycle will then lead to a continuation of the original problem. Only once the problem has been identified, and you are able to see why it is continuing, can you then think about how you would like things to be different. The changes you want to make can become your goals and you can become more focused in achieving these goals. This self-help guide will help you through that process.

The key ideas from CBT are:

- It is not what happens but how you interpret the experience that matters.
- How you think, or your beliefs about a situation or experience, will influence how you feel and behave.
- How you behave affects what you think and how you feel.
- Our thoughts, feelings, emotions and behaviors are all connected and each influences the other.

The key components of CBT treatment are:

- To identify and define your core problem(s) and how they influence your everyday life.
- Once a problem is defined, you need to identify the things that you do (or don't do) that lead to the problem continuing. These could include:
  - Unhelpful behaviors – for example, taking drugs or avoiding particular situations.
  - Negative thinking patterns – such as only focusing on the worst scenario.
  - Negative emotional states – like hopelessness or numbness.
  - Focusing on physical sensations – such as visual disturbances.
- You need to set out clear and specific changes that you would like to make. These then become the goals to work towards during CBT.
- The idea is then to actively work on achieving these goals using the variety of techniques set out in this book.

- Throughout this process you will be encouraged to evaluate your progress. This will involve recognizing what is working well and not so well. You can then draw up new goals to help you use what you've learned and apply this knowledge to other situations
- In essence, you will become your own therapist.

Introduction: Why a cognitive behavioral approach?

The approach this book takes in attempting to help you overcome your problems with depersonalization and feelings of unreality is a 'cognitive behavioral' one. A brief account of the history of this form of intervention is useful. In the 1950s and 1960s a set of therapeutic techniques was developed, collectively termed 'behavior therapy'. These techniques shared two basic features. First, they aimed to remove symptoms, such as anxiety, by dealing with those symptoms themselves, rather than their deep-seated, underlying historical causes (traditionally the focus of psychoanalysis, the approach developed by Sigmund Freud and his associates). Second, they were derived from what laboratory psychologists were discovering about the mechanisms of learning. Behavior therapy initially proved to be of most value in the treatment of anxiety disorders, especially specific phobias, such as extreme fear of animals or heights, and agoraphobia. Both were notoriously difficult to treat using conventional psychotherapies.

After an initial flush of enthusiasm, discontent with behavior therapy grew. There were a number of reasons for this. An important concern was the fact that behavior therapy did not deal with the internal thoughts which were so obviously central to the distress that many patients were experiencing. In particular, behavior therapy proved inadequate when it came to the treatment of depression. In the late 1960s and early 1970s a treatment for depression was developed called 'cognitive therapy'. The pioneer in this enterprise was an American psychiatrist, Professor Aaron T. Beck. He developed a theory of depression which emphasized the importance of people's depressed styles of thinking, and, on the basis of this theory, he specified a new form of therapy. It would not be an exaggeration to say that Beck's work has changed the nature of psychotherapy, not just for depression but for a range of psychological problems.

The techniques introduced by Beck have been merged with the techniques developed earlier by the behavior therapists to produce a therapeutic approach which has come to be known as 'cognitive behavioral therapy' (CBT). This therapy has been subjected to the strictest scientific testing and has been found to be highly successful for a significant proportion of cases of depression. It has now become clear that specific patterns of disturbed thinking are associated with a wide range of psychological problems, not just depression, and that CBT is a highly effective treatment for a range of anxiety disorders, such as panic disorder, generalized anxiety disorder, social phobia, obsessive compulsive disorder, and hypochondriasis (health anxiety), as well as for other conditions such as drug addictions, and eating disorders like bulimia nervosa. Indeed, cognitive behavioral techniques have been found to have an application beyond the narrow categories of psychological disorders. They have been applied effectively, for example, to helping sufferers of low self-esteem, people with weight problems, couples with marital difficulties, as well as those who wish to give up smoking or deal with drinking problems.

The starting point for CBT is the realization that the way we think, feel and behave are all intimately linked, and changing the way we think about ourselves, our experiences, and the world around us changes the way we feel and what we are able to do. So, for example, by helping a depressed person identify and challenge their automatic depressive thoughts, a route out of the cycle of depressive thoughts and feelings can be found. Similarly, habitual behavioral responses are driven by a complex set of thoughts and feelings, and CBT, by providing a means for the behavior to be brought under cognitive control, enables these responses to be undermined and a different kind of life to be possible.

Although effective CBT treatments have been developed for a wide range of disorders and problems, these treatments are not widely available. When people try on their own to help themselves, they often, inadvertently, do things which make matters worse. In recent years the community of cognitive behavioral therapists has responded to this situation. What they have done is to take the principles and techniques of specific cognitive behavioral therapies for particular problems and present them in manuals which people can read and apply themselves. These manuals specify a systematic program of treatment which the person works through to overcome their difficulties. In this way, cognitive behavioral therapeutic techniques of proven value are being made available to the widest possible readership.

The use of self-help manuals is never going to replace the need for therapists. Many people with emotional and behavioral problems will need the help of a qualified therapist. It is also the case that, despite the widespread success of cognitive behavioral therapy, some people will not respond to it and will need one of the other treatments available. Nevertheless, although research on the use of these self-help manuals is at an early stage, the work done to date indicates that for a great many people the use of a self-help manual is sufficient for them to overcome their problems without professional help. Sadly, many people suffer on their own for years. Sometimes they feel reluctant to seek help without first making a serious effort to manage on their own. Sometimes they feel too awkward or even ashamed to ask for help. Sometimes appropriate help is not forthcoming despite their efforts to find it. For many of these people the cognitive behavioral self-help manual will provide a lifeline to a better future.

Professor Peter J. Cooper
The University of Reading

PART ONE

Understanding DPAFU

1

What is DPAFU?

Descriptions of depersonalization and feelings of unreality started to appear in medical books and articles in the early nineteenth century, several decades before the condition was given a name.

Schilder, a German psychiatrist of the early twentieth century, gave one of the most detailed descriptions of depersonalization to date:

> To the depersonalized individual the world appears strange, peculiar, foreign, dream-like. Objects appear at times strangely diminished in size, at times flat. Sounds appear to come from a distance. The tactile characteristics of objects likewise seem strangely altered ... The emotions likewise undergo marked alteration. Patients complain that they are capable of experiencing neither pain nor pleasure; love and hate have perished with them. They experience a fundamental change in their personality, and the climax is reached with their complaints that they have become strangers to themselves. It is as though they were dead, lifeless, mere automatons ...

The term *derealization* was coined by an Irish psychiatrist, Edward Mapother, who was working at the Maudsley hospital between the wars. He used the term to refer to the way people's experience of their surroundings is odd or unusual (psychologists call this *altered feelings*). For example, occasionally people complain of visual distortion involving the size of objects, their three-dimensionality, or the sharpness of colours. Some people complain of an unearthly stillness in the world:

> *The world looks perfectly still like a postcard. It is standing still; there is no point in it. A bus moves along without purpose. It does not feel real. Everything in vision is dead; branches of trees are swaying without purpose.*

People with DPAFU often report that their actions feel robotic, as if they were on automatic pilot and 'spectators' of their own activities – like watching a movie or TV program of their own lives. Their voice may sound unfamiliar, and their thoughts, speech and actions no longer feel spontaneous. Sufferers also talk of an intense state of absorption in which they focus intently on these feelings. This state of absorption may in itself intensify the symptoms, leading to a vicious circle. Despite the fact that people with DPAFU feel they are robotic and on automatic pilot, this is often not noticeable or obvious to other people.

Another major factor in DPAFU is that sufferers describe an *inability to feel emotion*, even towards those close to them. On an intellectual level, you may be able to say that in circumstance 'A' you should feel happy and in circumstance 'B' you should feel sad, but in reality you may feel nothing whatsoever. As you can imagine, this is a very distressing experience and one that we will return to later on.

Many sufferers describe feeling as if *bodily changes* have taken place. Their head may feel strange, for example large or numb (people often say it's as if their head has been filled with cotton wool), or the body feels dead and lifeless. In some people this experience is so intense that they touch, punch or prick themselves repeatedly to try to feel 'normal' again.

Alongside these symptoms, there can be an additional feeling of being *cut off* from the world and even from one's own self. This can lead to doubts and confusion about one's own identity. For instance, sufferers often describe how their reflection in the mirror can seem unfamiliar to them. They fear lapsing into a void and losing their identity. Not surprisingly, people generally find it extremely difficult to describe these experiences, and usually use metaphors such as being *'in a dream'* or *'inside a bubble'*.

Lots of people affected with DPAFU also report significant levels of *anxiety*. This can take the form of panic attacks, a fear of going out alone, intense anxiety in social situations, or a tendency to worry too much. People with depression also report depersonalization from time to time, although it's generally confined to *emotional blunting* or *deadness of feeling* (as described above).

Some sufferers, however, are not visibly anxious or depressed but may be quite introverted or preoccupied. They spend a lot of time dwelling on their thoughts and may appear wrapped up in their own world. It's quite common for sufferers to spend excessive amounts of time worrying about abstract, existential, metaphysical, or hypochondriacal issues, such as the meanings of words, how other people experience the world, the meaning of life and concepts of space and time.

You may have noticed that the phrase 'as if' crops up a lot in these descriptions. This is very important because it shows that people don't say that, for example, they believe their head is actually full of cotton wool, or that they really are watching life go by on a film. It's just a way of trying to capture this weird experience and describe it to someone else. From the psychiatrist's or psychologist's point of view this is crucial. Saying 'as if' means that the experience is different from a delusion (a false belief) or a hallucination (when we perceive something that isn't really there) and so requires a different approach and different treatment.

How do I know if I have DPAFU?

Have a look at the checklist below that describes some of the main sensations associated with DPAFU. Put a tick next to each of the statements according to how often you experience these sensations in your everyday life.

CHECKLIST OF MAIN DPAFU SENSATIONS			
Main DPAFU sensations	Not at all	Yes, sometimes	Yes, definitely
Changes to feelings and emotions			
Feeling cut off or detached from the world around you			
Being emotionally numb			
Lacking empathy towards other people			
Feeling in a dream-like state			
Experiencing low mood			
Feeling like a robot or on 'automatic pilot'			
Experiencing anxiety			
Loss of motivation			
Feeling isolated from the world around you			
Not caring about your actions or behavior			

Checklist of main DPAFU sensations (cont.)

Main DPAFU sensations	Not at all	Yes, sometimes	Yes, definitely
Feeling like an observer of yourself			
Increased worry			
Problems with your thinking processes			
Finding it difficult to concentrate			
Feeling like your mind has 'gone blank'			
Experiencing thoughts that are speeded up and confused			
Having problems remembering everyday things			
Feeling detached from past memories			
Having difficulty picturing things in your mind's eye			
Struggling to take in new information			
Unusual physical and perceptual sensations			
The world around you appears unreal or artificial			
Physical numbness in parts or all of your body			
Feelings of weightlessness or hollowness			
Losing your sense of taste, touch or smell			
Objects around you appearing smaller than they really are			

Checklist of main DPAFU sensations (cont.)

Main DPAFU sensations	Not at all	Yes, sometimes	Yes, definitely
Objects around you appearing larger than they really are			
Experiencing distortions to sounds (including your own voice)			
The world around you appearing less colourful than it really is			
Feeling dizzy or losing your balance			
Objects and the world around you appearing flat or two-dimensional			
Objects seeming not to be solid			
Feeling detached from your own reflection when looking in a mirror			
Feeling as if time has been slowed down or speeded up			

If your responses to the statements above are mainly 'yes, sometimes' or 'yes, definitely', we think this book can make a big contribution to your efforts to overcome DPAFU. Your answers will show which DPAFU sensations are specific to you. This information will come in useful later on when you start to use the CBT strategies we describe in subsequent chapters.

When does DPAFU occur?

Lasting or severe experiences of DPAFU are often reported in people who have a wide range of mental health problems.

These can include agoraphobia (where people feel too frightened to leave their home), Obsessive Compulsive Disorder (where people are plagued by intrusive thoughts, for example the belief that they are dirty or contaminated, and have a compulsion to act on them, in this instance by constantly washing their hands), health anxiety (also known as hypochondriasis), social anxiety (where people are very frightened of being with other people in everyday social situations) and excessive worrying. The sensations of DPAFU are particularly common in people who have panic attacks, with up to 34 per cent of people reporting DPAFU during their attacks. DPAFU is also often associated with people who have depression or continually low mood. DPAFU sensations can also occur during, and immediately following, a very traumatic experience such as a road traffic accident or a natural disaster.

As DPAFU sensations can often occur alongside other psychological or emotional conditions, clinicians used to believe it led to psychosis (the most serious kind of mental illness). It is in fact very rare for DPAFU to lead to psychosis, which instead involves very different sensations i.e. hallucinations and delusions. There is no evidence that persistent depersonalization, in which sufferers describe their experience using the crucial words *as if*, has any relationship to schizophrenia or any other psychotic illness.

Depersonalization can also be a symptom of neurological conditions such as temporal lobe epilepsy and migraine headaches. As a general rule, this kind of depersonalization is fleeting and associated with other, very different symptoms such as seizures and complete loss of consciousness.

There are a few more situations that can lead to DPAFU. People who have recently been bereaved often experience many of the symptoms of DPAFU. However, these symptoms tend to disappear within four to six weeks, although they can occasionally last longer. Some people also experience depersonalization when they take hallucinogenic drugs such as cannabis, ketamine or Ecstasy and they start to have unusual experiences or feel very 'speeded up'. Most commonly of all though, people report short-lived states of depersonalization when tired, jet-lagged, under severe stress, during deep relaxation or after an intense emotional experience. Given those reasons, it's hardly surprising that DPAFU is often reported by women after childbirth.

Diagnosing DPAFU

Depersonalization is described in the American handbook of psychiatric conditions, the *Diagnostic and Statistical Manual of the American Psychiatric Association*, Version IV (1994), known as DSM-IV for short, as:

> ... *an alteration in the perception or experience of the self so that one feels detached from, and as if one is an outside observer of, one's mental processes or body (e.g. feeling like one is in a dream).*

Derealization is defined as 'an alteration in the perception or experience of the external world so that it seems strange or unreal' (e.g. people may seem unfamiliar or mechanical). According to DSM-IV, a diagnosis of depersonalization disorder is made when the following four criteria are met:

- Persistent or recurrent experiences of feeling detached from, and as if one is an outside observer of, one's mental processes or body; e.g. feeling like one is in a dream.

- During the depersonalization experience, reality testing remains intact (i.e. you are aware that it 'feels as if you are unreal' but know that this is just a feeling and it is not really the case).
- The depersonalization causes clinically significant distress or impairment in social, occupational or other important areas of functioning, for example if someone is so distressed that they cannot carry out day-to-day living.
- The depersonalization experience is not part of another disorder.

The 10th revision of the World Health Organization's *International Classification of Diseases* (ICD-10), an alternative handbook that is used widely by clinicians in Europe for diagnosis, describes depersonalization/derealization syndrome as:

A feeling of being distant, not really here. For example, individuals may complain that their emotions, feelings, or experiences of the inner self are detached, strange, not their own, or unpleasantly lost, or that their emotions or movements seem as if they belong to someone else, or that they feel as if they were acting in a play.

As with DSM-IV, according to ICD-10 the affected person needs to realize that their DPAFU only reflects their feelings about the world – and not the way the world really is. Depersonalization disorder is only diagnosed if the person has this as their main problem and not merely as a part of another problem, such as depression.

If the descriptions above appear to fit with how you have been feeling and/or you do not already have the diagnosis of DPAFU, it may be useful for your future treatment to see your GP and discuss these feelings. You may wish to take this section of the book along with you. Many of the people we see report that their GP knew very little about their condition and we know that it is not unusual to be misdiagnosed with other conditions. Your GP may want to refer you to a psychiatrist to gain a better understanding of your problems if they are having a significant effect on you.

There are also a number of rating scales used mostly in research to quantify symptoms and track changes with treatment. One scale designed specifically for DPAFU is the Cambridge Depersonalization Scale (see Appendix I). This comes in two versions: a 'state' version that rates how you're feeling right now; and a 'trait' version that rates how you have been feeling over the past six months. Another widely used scale which covers DPAFU along with other similar and associated symptoms is the Dissociative Experiences Scale (see p. 230).

In addition, having DPAFU does not prevent you from feeling other psychological symptoms. Occasionally people who report DPAFU also suffer from depression and anxiety, and through reading this book you may become aware of other such problems. If so, we would urge you to go along to your GP and seek further help. On the other hand, you may come to the conclusion that what you have experienced is not as worrying or as serious as you had feared initially, and feel that there is no need for additional help.

How common is DPAFU?

You might be very surprised to discover just how common the sensations of DPAFU are. Indeed, when members of the public are surveyed the vast majority report that they have experienced DPAFU for brief periods of time. One study found that just over 70 per cent of people reported experiencing DPAFU at some point in their life. It is more common in younger rather than older adults. Another recent random telephone survey in the US found that nearly a quarter of people questioned had had periods of DPAFU during the last year alone. Luckily, more severe DPAFU is less common. Nevertheless, a survey of people in South London, again randomly selected but then interviewed face-to-face, found that up to 2 per cent had DPAFU that was severe enough to be causing distress and significantly affecting their life. These figures are equivalent to those for other common problems such as Obsessive Compulsive Disorder (OCD).

The figures increase when the interviews involve people who have mental health problems or have been through traumatic events. For example, up to two thirds of people who survived life-threatening danger stated that they had DPAFU at the time of their trauma. In addition, those who have diagnoses of depression, anxiety or other mental health difficulties report high rates of DPAFU alongside their other symptoms. Some of the highest rates of DPAFU are in those people who have anxiety problems, especially those who experience panic attacks.

Overall, the results of these various surveys show that DPAFU is not rare. Temporary sensations of DPAFU are widespread in the general population. More severe DPAFU is much less common but still as common as some other well-known conditions such as OCD.

Is there a typical DPAFU pattern?

There is no single type of person who experiences DPAFU, nor is there a set pattern for the way the condition arises or develops. However, studies have looked at large numbers of people reporting recurring DPAFU and have found some general trends. First, equal numbers of men and women seem to experience DPAFU. This is an interesting result because anxiety and depression tend to be much more common in women. People often first experience DPAFU in the period from their late teens to their mid-twenties, although there are significant numbers who report their first experience much later than this.

Second, there seem to be three main ways in which sensations of DPAFU first start. Some people describe a sudden onset i.e. one day it was just there. The sensations then remain at roughly the same severity over time. Others mention that they started with short periods of DPAFU that became longer until the DPAFU became continual (i.e. present all the time) or recurrent (i.e. coming back after periods of being absent). Lastly, some people feel that they have always had some DPAFU, although they were perhaps unaware of this until a later date.

Around 75 per cent of people with continual or recurrent DPAFU experience both a sense of unreality about themselves *and* the world around them. A smaller proportion experience feelings of unreality just about themselves. Approximately 5 per cent of people have only a sense of unreality about the outside world.

In the next chapter, we present three case studies of people affected by DPAFU. They provide an excellent illustration of the different patterns of DPAFU and the influence these experiences can have on someone's life.

2

DPAFU case studies

This chapter presents the stories of three people dealing with DPAFU. Their experiences, and their backgrounds, are all very different. For example the first person, Jay, believed DPAFU started after illicit drug-taking. The second person, Mina, believed that DPAFU started for no apparent reason. Alexi, whose story is the third featured here, was a life-long sufferer who only became aware of DPAFU through listening to a radio program.

As you'll see from these case studies, DPAFU affects people in a variety of ways. It may be that you're able to identify with one case more than another or that you feel that bits from all of the case studies are relevant to you. If you feel that you have nothing in common with any of the cases you may wish to read the diagnostic criteria (see page 10) and check whether a diagnosis of DPAFU is the right one for you. You should also talk to your GP.

Jay

Jay is a 25-year-old man. He did well at secondary school and was a popular and able pupil, if a little shy, gaining good grades. He went to university to study history. During his first year he found the transition to university hard. He missed home, which surprised him, and found he was no longer an 'A' grade student. He did however have a good social life and a wide circle of friends. One night at a party he took some Ecstasy and later smoked some cannabis (something he had done in the past but not often). But this time he noticed something different about the quality of the experience. He had an overwhelming sense of fear, and later panic, and desperately wanted the drugs out of his system. He remembers feeling 'spaced out and detached'. He went to bed to sleep it off but when he woke the next day he still felt 'odd'. The drugs did not appear to have affected any of his friends in quite the same way. He wondered if the drugs had been spiked or if they had caused some sort of brain damage. He became increasingly aware over the next few months of feeling 'not right'. He had weird visual sensations of a dulling of brightness. It felt as if he was watching life on a video screen. Things no longer appeared to bother him, and he felt as if he had no emotion at all – 'just nothing; it was like being emotionally numb'. Jay went to his college GP and was prescribed antidepressants. But instead of helping him, they just made him feel more anxious. He went back to his GP and was prescribed anxiety medication but this just made him feel more 'spaced out'. He avoided situations where he thought people would scrutinize him, such as going to dinner parties, and travelled on the train in a separate compartment. Jay became increasingly aware of thoughts that went round and round in his head and that he couldn't get rid of no matter how hard he tried. These thoughts were centred on issues such as the meaning of life, who we are as human beings and our purpose in life. When he looked in the mirror he was unsure of who he saw in the reflection. On an intellectual level he knew it was himself, but on an emotional level it did not feel like him. He went back to his GP, and also went to see the college counsellor. Discussing things with the counsellor helped, but she was only able to see Jay for six sessions and he could not afford to see a private therapist.

Jay found it increasingly difficult to manage at university. He passed his degree, albeit with a lower mark than he expected. He returned to the family home, went back to his GP and was referred to a local psychiatrist. Jay became very anxious about the meaning of his symptoms. He believed that the psychiatrist would think he was 'really' mad and was afraid that he might be experiencing the early symptoms of schizophrenia. Over the next four years Jay was prescribed a wide variety of medicines but none ever took away the odd feelings that he found so difficult to put into words. He tried to explain exactly how he felt to friends and family but felt that he was never really understood. It was only through an Internet search that he became aware that other people felt a similar way and found out about our Depersonalisation Research Unit. Here he was treated with a combination of medication and cognitive behavioral therapy (CBT). He still has some sensations associated with DPAFU most of the time, but they no longer worry him. He is currently working part-time for the civil service.

Mina

Mina described herself as a normal child who had a happy childhood. She grew up in a small town in a rural area. She said that she felt close to her parents, particularly her mother. She had a younger sister and brother. She did well at school and had plenty of friends and boyfriends. After college she built a good career in management. She had a good relationship with her boyfriend and was planning her wedding. All was going well in life until, when aged 27, her mother developed a terminal illness. She moved back home to help her father cope and nursed her mother until she died. As planned, Mina then married and moved to the other side of town with her new husband. They spent the next couple of years renovating the new house and set up a business together. They would have described themselves as a happy newly wed couple with a bright future ahead of them.

Then, out of the blue, she began to notice a strange feeling when in the company of others. She said it was like being an observer on the outside and looking in. She felt in no way connected to any other people, including her husband, at these times. She then began to have doubts about whether or not people that she knew actually liked her or whether they felt sorry for her or only liked her because of her husband. She began to dwell on her childhood and how lonely and isolated she had felt. Mina began to avoid social gatherings including her beloved art classes. She became aware that on some days the strange feelings she experienced when others were present began to happen when she was alone. She felt detached from herself and in fact said that she no longer knew who she was. At times she felt as if she would 'disappear' and she would pinch herself because the pain made her feel more real. Familiar places and locations took on an unreal quality. For instance, when driving she felt as if she was experiencing the world through a sheet of muslin – she felt cut off from the outside world. She felt that she had no control over her actions and that she had become almost robotic. Her voice did not sound like her own and her hands sometimes appeared to distort in size and image. She believed that she had gone completely mad. But then the next day the sensations would pass, or she would not be aware of them, and things would feel better.

Over a period of a year things got better until no sensations of DPAFU were present. Then, out of the blue, the sensations returned and remained constant. Mina tried to make sense of what was happening to her. There did not appear to be any logical reason why the symptoms should return now. Mina, like Jay, had found out about our Unit from the Internet and she asked her GP to refer her. She refused to take any medication, but undertook a course of CBT. During the treatment she began to have 'flashes' of reality where very briefly all of her symptoms disappeared. These episodes of reality were enough to reassure her that eventually she would feel well enough to be able to live life as she had hoped and expected. One year on, Mina is free from the sensations of DPAFU but remains reluctant to think of herself as cured.

Alexi

Alexi is a 56-year-old man. After listening to a radio program he realized that the description of DPAFU matched perfectly how he had felt all of his life. He had been aware of always feeling a bit detached from other people and himself, and places often had an unreal quality to them. In fact he said that he was 'disconnected' from everything including himself. He attributed his feelings to having moved around the world a lot as a child when his father was in the military, and that he had not really formed any 'connections'. But having felt this way for as long as he could remember, he really did not have anything to compare it with. He believed that other people experienced things differently from him, but again had no way of knowing for sure. He felt that he was only 'half living life'. Alexi often felt very low in mood, especially when he thought about the love he had for his wife and children. For him, his love was false because, while he could say on an intellectual level that he loved them, he never felt it emotionally. Life really did feel like it was just a process of going through the motions. He had tried in the past to talk to his wife about how he felt, but she always became upset when he spoke of his 'lack' of feelings for her and their family. He made a conscious decision not to talk about it anymore. For

Alexi, life was 'one big act'. He said that he knew on a mental level what to do, what to say, and how he was supposed to feel, but he never truly 'felt' it. He described himself as being 'numb' inside.

Following a referral to the Unit, he began a combination of cognitive behavioral therapy and antidepressant medication to help him manage his low mood. During treatment he became aware of aspects of his life that were 'unrewarding' and 'unfulfilling'. Towards the end of therapy he decided he would change direction in his work. Instead of working in the lucrative private sector he chose to work in a less well-paid job for a local charity.

Six months later Alexi returned to the Unit. He said that he continued to experience sensations of 'emotional numbness' but somehow it was more bearable. His feeling of DPAFU continued to a lesser degree. He believed that the sensations he experienced had less of an impact on his life.

3

A brief history of DPAFU

Descriptions of the symptoms of depersonalization disorder have appeared in books since the early nineteenth century, several decades before the condition was given a name. For example, an early letter written by a patient described her symptoms as follows:

> I continue to suffer constantly . . . My existence is incomplete. The functions and acts of ordinary life, it is true, still remain to me; but in every one of them there is something lacking. That is, the sensation which is proper to them . . . Each of my senses, each part of my proper self is as if it were separated from me and can no longer afford me any sensation.

The name depersonalization was suggested by Ludovic Dugas, a French psychologist, at the end of the nineteenth century. It was intended to describe 'a state in which the feelings or sensations which normally accompany mental activity seem absent from the self; there is an alienation of the self; in other words a *depersonalization*'. Dugas thought that depersonalization reflected an abnormality of a normal mental function he called 'personalization'.

Early theories proposed that depersonalization was caused by a physical or neurological disorder. Doctors believed they were unable to identify the exact nature of the condition due to unsophisticated equipment and lack of technology. Others argued that depersonalization was really just an absence of emotional feelings. Later ideas drew attention to the fact that depersonalization is commonly associated with anxiety or feelings of being under threat, as seen for example in the accounts of people who were imprisoned in concentration camps and of survivors of other traumas such as road traffic accidents. This association was seen as suggesting that depersonalization served as a protective mechanism. Given the fact that extreme states of anxiety can cloud judgement and lead to reckless behavior, it was proposed that depersonalization served to dampen down such potentially disruptive emotions.

The following case provides a good illustration of the way depersonalization can work to protect us:

A man was driving at some speed on a wet road and, as he turned a corner, the car skidded. He immediately experienced a dream-like detachment and found himself steering mechanically. He was also aware of his actions as if he were viewing some other unfortunate victim from a distance. After spinning round several times, and narrowly avoiding oncoming traffic, the car finally came to a halt facing in the opposite direction. The driver felt quite calm but when the bystanders spoke to him their voices seemed muffled and the surrounding countryside appeared still, remote and unreal. His own voice also sounded unfamiliar. He drove on feeling quite calm and arrived at work. After a few minutes of being involved in his daily activities, his depersonalization suddenly lifted and he became aware that he was perspiring, trembling severely and his heart was pounding at a rapid rate.

Such theories didn't really explain how some cases of depersonalization become long-lasting – once the anxiety or threat had gone, you would expect that the DPAFU should disappear as well. But long-lasting cases were believed to be the manifestation of an accompanying psychiatric condition such as depression. Such was the view proposed by the German psychiatrist Mayer-Gross. He viewed depersonalization as a symptom that could be triggered by a whole range of different neurological or psychiatric conditions. In 1946, H. J. Shorvon, an eminent British psychiatrist, disagreed with this view and suggested that there was a distinct group of patients who appeared to experience the symptoms of depersonalization with no other discernible psychiatric cause. However, the fact that patients with long-lasting depersonalization also suffered from anxiety led the psychiatrist Sir Martin Roth to suggest that depersonalization may be an anxiety condition and he came up with the name 'phobic-anxiety-depersonalization syndrome'. Like earlier writers, he suggested that depersonalization may have been intended by nature as a form of coping mechanism to help us deal with extreme situations.

Unfortunately, for most of the second half of the twentieth century there was much less interest in depersonalization. It became almost accepted that severe depersonalization was extremely rare, and that when it was experienced, it occurred as an almost irrelevant symptom of another condition such as depression or schizophrenia. Not surprisingly, such assumptions had a negative effect on the amount of research being done, and it is fair to say that up until the mid-1990s our understanding of this condition had changed little since 1950. Fortunately, this gloomy scenario has dramatically changed over the past fifteen years following renewed interest in the condition. There have been major advances on several fronts. Larger than ever numbers of patients with depersonalization disorder have now been carefully studied, resulting in a thorough tracking of the clinical manifestations and clinical course of the condition. New questionnaires designed to detect and gauge the severity of the condition have been created, which have allowed doctors to make a more accurate diagnosis of the condition. In turn, this has also enabled more rigorous research into DPAFU. In fact, for the first time doctors are beginning to understand the mechanisms in the brain, which are involved in depersonalization. Recent large-scale surveys of the general population are also starting to reveal that, far from being a rare condition, depersonalization disorder may in fact be as common as well-known psychiatric conditions such as schizophrenia or manic depressive illness. Lastly, but not least, the last decade has seen important advances in both the psychological and pharmacological (i.e. drug-based) treatment of this condition.

4

What causes DPAFU?

Physical explanations: What does the brain have to do with it?

In keeping with other researchers, we think that depersonalization represents the activity of a *protective 'reflex of the mind'*, or an automatic response, which is usually activated in threatening situations where the individual does not seem to have any control. We believe that this mechanism inhibits the 'emotional' brain, in order to protect the individual from the confusing effect that extreme levels of anxiety can have on our mind and behavior. For instance, it is known that at high levels of anxiety people can act in a reckless manner. This only hampers our ability to cope with threatening situations.

Here's an example. Picture someone involved in a very traumatic, life-threatening incident such as a natural disaster. In this situation, a person may feel so terrified and over-whelmed that they are unable to think coherently, protect themselves or escape. Imagine instead what would happen if they were able to become 'emotionally numb' for a short period. This might be much more helpful. Rather than becoming overwhelmed and unable to function, they would be able to act calmly and leave the situation. However, they may also have a sense of unreality and feel as though they are in a dream, both during the experience and for some time afterwards.

It is possible to scan and take images of the brain while a person is experiencing certain feelings or trying to do various tasks. This shows which bits of the brain are or are not working – or are working too much or too little. Recent brain-imaging findings show that a group of brain structures known as the 'limbic system' (also known as the 'emotional brain' and made up of parts of the temporal lobes and deep structures in the front and centre of the brain all connected together in a kind of circuit) play an important role in labelling the things we perceive with emotional significance. This 'emotional tag' determines the type of emotions we experience in response to situations, objects and people around us, but also colours the way we perceive and experience things. So in addition to knowing or recognizing the things we see or hear around us (knowing that this object in front of me is a tree, a person, a telephone etc.), we also have a feeling of 'emotional recognition' (I like this object; I recognize this person; that thing frightens me, etc.). This in turn determines our feelings of being part of the world, and the way we experience reality. Any disruption in this process could lead to a significant change in the way we experience ourselves and our surroundings – it could, in other words, lead to feelings of unreality.

Brain imaging studies have shown that people with depersonalization disorder do not show the usual level of activity in the emotional brain when they look at unpleasant pictures. Likewise, the bodily responses that indicate emotional arousal (an example would be sweating) are unusually small and slow in people with depersonalization. Some work has also suggested that the hormones that are usually released into the blood stream in response to stress (such as cortisol) are also reduced in people with depersonalization – although not all laboratories find this pattern. All in all, this evidence seems to suggest that people with depersonalization disorder have an oversensitive emotion-suppressing mechanism. This may be because the mechanism was put to use early on in their lives, or because it was triggered by stress or a drug. Or maybe some people are just born this way. No one really knows.

We think that this 'protective' depersonalization response was intended by nature to be brief, and for it to last only as long as the perceived threat (as in the above example of a life-threatening trauma). However, in people with continual and recurring sensations of DPAFU this response becomes persistent and unhelpful. We have also gathered evidence that suggests that giving what psychologists call a 'catastrophic meaning' to this temporary response (e.g. 'There must be something wrong with my brain'; 'I must be going mad' etc.) can lead to it continuing. DPAFU itself then becomes a threatening event, which triggers more DPAFU and so on, setting up a vicious circle that maintains the condition.

Psychological explanations: What does the mind have to do with it?

In the previous section we looked at the physical explanation of DPAFU. There are also psychological explanations of DPAFU that focus on the mind and behavior. For example, ideas about how we learn, how we interpret our experiences, the ways in which we change our behavior, our different moods, memory and attention are all important. Also important are our ideas about the world and what health and illness mean to us as individuals. These physical and psychological perspectives are not mutually exclusive and are very much interrelated.

In psychological terms, the starting point is a set or group of *sensations* or experiences.

SENSATIONS

cut off, unreal, spaced out, visual disturbances, numb

As we described earlier, these sensations are not in themselves out of the ordinary. In fact, they are common to most people under certain circumstances – for example, feeling 'spaced out' and 'cut off' when you have a hangover; seeing 'floaters' or 'spots' before the eyes or experiencing the world as somehow 'surreal, flat or lifeless' when you are tired. It is the sense you make of these sensations, rather than the sensations themselves, that can have a big impact upon your responses. If, for example, you attribute the sensations to nothing more than a hangover, feeling tired or being under stress, then you are content that you have an explanation for how you are feeling and tend not to give the matter much more thought. If on the other hand you are uncertain as to the cause, or become worried about what these sensations mean, then you may begin to give the matter more thought and generate a variety of possible explanations.

Remember that at this stage you don't know that these sensations or experiences could be called depersonalization disorder, so you're busy trying to make sense of what's happening. If your explanations or *appraisals* tend towards the 'negative' or the 'sinister' – for example, if you believe that 'these feelings are the early signs of schizophrenia or a brain tumour' or are the result of taking illicit drugs, then it's natural to *worry* more. This will mean you pay more attention to the experiences and what is happening inside your body (see Figure 4.1).

When you pay more attention to what is happening inside your body, you're paying far less attention to what is happening *on the outside*. This can lead to a change in how you

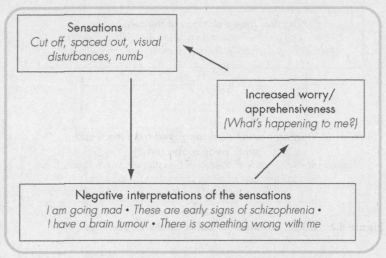

Figure 4.1   Initial links between feelings and thoughts

experience this external reality, which can in turn lead you to feel 'cut off' or 'detached' from the world, yourself and others. Imagine that your short-term memory has a limited capacity. It can only process 100 units and you are using 30 units on processing what is happening inside your body, i.e. checking out how you're feeling inside. This would mean you only have 70 units left to process the outside world. It's not surprising then that you may at times feel a bit cut off, or that your concentration is poor, or that your attention span is not what it was beforehand. Any one of these experiences could then result in you worrying more.

It is often difficult to attend to both your inner and exterior world at the same time, even if you think you can multi-task! When we look at the example above, it's easy to see how the very fact that you become increasingly worried or *apprehensive* about the meaning of these sensations can lead to a negative cycle. The usual or 'normal' sensations of anxiety

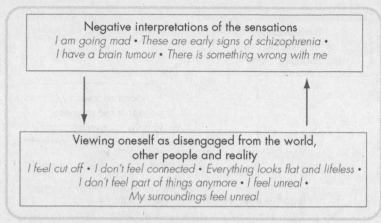

Figure 4.2   Initial attempts to make sense of feelings

are now added to the sensations of DPAFU you are already feeling. This can then give rise to thoughts about the self as feeling 'cut off' or *disengaged* from the world and/or other people. When we feel disengaged, we can also feel that our sense of reality is reduced (see Figure 4.2), either in relation to the self (depersonalization) and/or the world around us (derealization).

The way in which you interpret or 'make sense' of these sensations also depends on many other factors, such as your ideas and beliefs. Many of our ideas and central or core beliefs arise from the experiences we have as children and adults. These beliefs and ideas form sets of rules on the basis of which we make assumptions (see Figure 4.3 opposite).

Our core beliefs are in operation in everyday life, for instance in the way we think of ourselves in relation to others, and in our general approach to life, i.e. happy-go-lucky versus pessimistic. Our beliefs are influenced by the values of our culture and society, as well as our ideas about what constitutes health and illness. It is very likely that you

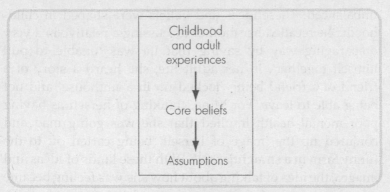

Figure 4.3   Influences on current thinking

will have an idea of what it means (for you) to be 'healthy' or 'sane'. So if something should come along to challenge these beliefs then it is likely that you will think of yourself as 'ill'.

Given that you have probably learned over time that feeling a certain way (like feeling emotionally numb) or having certain thoughts ('who am I?', 'I don't feel real') is 'not usual', you will naturally want to understand what is happening to you. If these feelings and/or thoughts last, you may interpret these sensations as meaning you have a medical condition like a disease or abnormality of the brain or the beginnings of a mental illness. The experience of these sensations will then probably lead you to assume that you're ill or that something is very wrong.

We can illustrate this point by thinking back to Mina's story (see page 17). She held a set of ideas or core beliefs about the importance of good health, especially mental health, and what that meant to her. Any deviation away from those core beliefs had important implications for her. She believed very strongly that good mental health was a sign of a strong, well-balanced person. Her assumption was that if you do not have good mental health then you are weak and unbalanced. These ideas and beliefs were shaped in child-hood. She recalled her mother discussing a relative in a very disparaging way by saying that he was 'unable to pull himself together'. In her adult life, she heard a story of a friend of a friend being 'locked up in a nuthouse' and not being able to leave. For Mina, thinking of herself as having poor mental health implied that she was going mad and conjured up the image of herself 'being carted off to the funny farm in a straightjacket'. With these kinds of ideas and images, the idea of talking about how she was feeling became a further source of anxiety, worry and led to a low mood. Mina was frightened she would be labelled mad.

As you learn more about what is happening to you and come to label or call it DPAFU, you will probably develop some specific interpretations or explanations. With any per-ceived alteration in your state of being it's usual to pay close attention to how exactly you're feeling. You then begin or continue to monitor carefully the sensations or signs and symptoms associated with the condition. In fact it is likely that you begin to attribute *all* sensations that you can't make sense of to the condition. It's also probable that you aren't consciously aware of this process, just the end result of being intensely aware of your inner state. However, this *increased symptom monitoring* is likely to exacerbate your perception of both the frequency and severity of these sensations and so contribute to the worsening vicious cycle.

This can make you very sensitive to how you're feeling, especially if you also think about how things used to be, and focus on how you imagine things are for other people. Unsurprisingly, these interpretations can often lead to low mood and increased anxiety or worry. Increased awareness of your thoughts and feelings can result in a negative cycle and deepen the distressing feelings associated with DPAFU. If this condition or pattern of experience then causes further

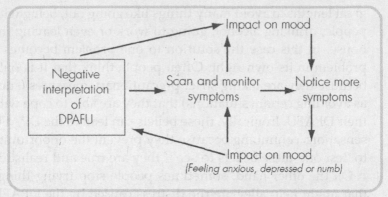

Figure 4.4 Links between thoughts, mood and sensations

distress or disability, you'll feel even worse about your condition and *specific negative interpretations of DPAFU* will follow (see Figure 4.4).

If we feel discomfort or distress it is natural to try to find behaviors, thoughts, situations or substances to take away those unpleasant feelings. This could be through pretending to act normal, avoiding certain things like looking at yourself in the mirror (or doing them all the time), or distracting yourself from your thoughts. You may stop drinking alcohol because being drunk and/or hungover intensifies the sensations associated with DPAFU. You may also find yourself saying positive things inside your head like: 'I am real, this is me' or trying to do more of the things that are known to improve other conditions, such as relaxation, a healthy diet and exercise. Any action that is used to take away distress or discomfort and to make yourself feel better is called a *safety-seeking behavior*. These behaviors can appear very useful in the short term, but they tend not to last or can actually make the situation worse in the long term.

Another common strategy to help cope with feelings of DPAFU is *avoidance*. For example, you could end up going to great lengths to avoid many things like going out, being with people, drinking alcohol, going to work or even leaving the house. In this case the solution to one problem becomes a problem in its own right. Often people think that it is only because they are taking strict precautionary measures (such as avoiding certain situations) that they are able to cope with their DPAFU. Ironically, these beliefs can lead to the DPAFU sensations continuing because they prevent the opportunity to 'test out' these beliefs to see if they are true and realistic.

On the other hand, sometimes people stop trying things that might help alleviate the distress caused by the DPAFU sensations. This then leads to an overwhelming sense that nothing works and it is all hopeless. When (and if) you feel this way, your mood lowers and you may feel depressed. Either way it is important to learn to identify both the *safety-seeking behaviors* and *avoidances* that you're using. Otherwise, they could continue to perpetuate the negative cycles that maintain the problems associated with DPAFU. For example, even positive safety-seeking behaviors such as giving up alcohol can become a negative cycle that maintains the DPAFU if, say, you become increasingly anxious about having a drink and/or begin to actively avoid doing so (see Figure 4.5 opposite).

Linking body and mind

We have talked about the physical explanations of DPAFU. We've seen how what happens in the brain may lead to the particular sensations that are associated with DPAFU, i.e. feeling cut off, unreal, spaced out. We've also looked at psychological explanations, which detail how our thoughts and behavior in response to DPAFU can lead to these sensations becoming problematic for us. In this section we'll briefly summarize how the body (physical factors) and mind

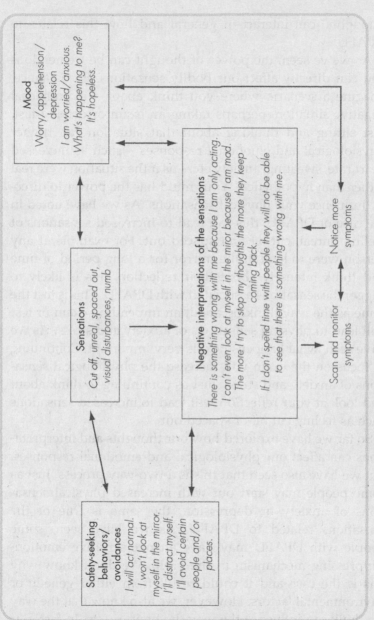

Mood
Worry/apprehension/
depression
I am worried/anxious.
What's happening to me?
It's hopeless.

Sensations
Cut off, unreal, spaced out,
visual disturbances, numb

Negative interpretations of the sensations
There is something wrong with me because I am only acting.
I can't even look at myself in the mirror because I am mad.
The more I try to stop my thoughts the more they keep
coming back.
If I don't spend time with people they will not be able
to see that there is something wrong with me.

Notice more
symptoms

Scan and monitor
symptoms

**Safety-seeking
behaviors/
avoidances**
I will act normal.
I won't look at
myself in the mirror.
I'll distract myself.
I'll avoid certain
people and/or
places.

Figure 4.5 Linking thoughts, mood, sensations and behavior

(thoughts) can interact in general and how this relates to DPAFU.

As we've seen, the power of thought can be tremendous and can directly affect our bodily sensations. For instance, imagine a scenario where you think about a hypothetical negative situation, perhaps taking an exam or driving test. Just sitting and thinking about that situation can trigger physiological and emotional responses – such as increased heart rate, sweating, anxiety etc. – as if the situation were real rather than hypothetical. Your mind has the power to directly influence your physical sensations. As we have noted in the case of DPAFU, this can lead to increased sensations of feeling unreal, cut off and spaced out. For example, if any person were to look in the mirror for a long period of time and think intensely about their reflection, this is likely to trigger the sensations associated with DPAFU. This is just the same as the way thinking about an impending exam or test will lead to physical sensations of anxiety and stress. As we have seen, what happens next is very important. Continuing to focus on the exam will increase the physiological sensations of anxiety and stress, just as continuing to think about and look at your reflection will lead to increased sensations such as feeling cut off or spaced out.

So far we have explored how our thoughts and interpretations can affect our physiological and emotional responses. But we have also seen that this is a two-way process. Just as some people may start out with increased physical sensations of anxiety or depression, the same is true of the sensations related to DPAFU. As we have seen, some people with DPAFU may have an oversensitive emotion-suppressing mechanism in the brain. We don't know why this is the case and it could result from either genetic or environmental factors. However, we also know that the way we think can influence the way the brain reacts. In fact, our thoughts, actions and experiences are so powerful that they can modify our actual brain structures even when we're adults. The interaction between the mind and brain is very complex, and we know that the brain is very changeable. For instance, one scientific study shows that twelve people who learned to juggle over three months actually changed the structure and shape of their brain.

In summary, just as the body can affect the mind, so too can the mind have an impact on the body. Both physical and psychological explanations for DPAFU are important and interact with each other. This means that even if you believe strongly that your DPAFU has a physical explanation, working with your thoughts and behavior using the CBT techniques we describe in this book is likely to have a positive impact on your physical symptoms of DPAFU.

CHAPTER SUMMARY

DPAFU can affect you on five levels:

1 **Cognitive** – thoughts, beliefs, meanings, images, attention and memory.

2 **Emotional** – how you feel, your moods, numbness.

3 **Behavioral** – what you do more or less of, things you avoid.

4 **Physical** – bodily changes, sleep patterns, numbness.

5 **Environmental** – situations, relationships, work, home.

To help you to identify the ways in which DPAFU affects you personally on each of these levels, write a list under each of the headings. This will be useful in the subsequent chapters when you start to use the CBT techniques we present to help you manage your DPAFU and the problems associated with it.

1 Cognitive i.e. thoughts, beliefs, meanings, etc.
For example, 'I think there is something wrong with my brain.

2 Emotional i.e. how you feel, your mood etc.
For example, 'I feel like I have no emotions.

3 Behavioral i.e. what do you do more or less of, things you avoid.
For example, 'I don't go out anymore in case people think I'm weird.

4 Physical i.e. what sensations you have inside your body.
For example, 'I see floaters in front of my eyes.

5 Environmental i.e. external factors such as alcohol, sleep, exercise.
For example, 'I had to give up my job because I felt spaced out all of the time.

PART TWO

Overcoming DPAFU

5

The cognitive behavioral therapy approach: CBT for DPAFU

Introduction

The treatment options under the heading of 'psychological' can include many different approaches, from individual therapy with a psychologist or counsellor, through to reading self-help books and practising relaxation at home. In this and the following chapter we will look at CBT, which is the main psychological approach that has been found to benefit people with DPAFU. Psychological approaches can be combined with medication or other treatments. In fact such combinations are usually the best option for people who have more severe symptoms. Using psychological approaches does not mean that there is nothing physical or physiological (i.e. relating to the body) about DPAFU. In fact, as we discussed in the last chapter, separating 'physical' and 'mental' sensations is old-fashioned and often unhelpful.

The CBT approach

Cognitive behavioral therapy (CBT) or cognitive therapy (CT) is a type of talking therapy that has been found to be very effective at treating a wide range of problems, including anxiety, depression, low self-esteem, anger, trauma, eating problems and relationship difficulties. It is not especially concerned with your childhood or your fantasy life but focuses instead on your thinking styles and what happens here and now. CBT and CT come from the same origins; namely an American psychiatrist called Professor Aaron T. Beck, who worked to develop a talking therapy for depression in the late 1960s.

Beck noticed that depressed patients had a particular way of thinking about themselves and others, the world and the future. He observed a tendency towards a negative style of processing information – the glass was always half empty, never half full. He saw that negative patterns in thinking styles were very common and that they often included some kind of negative bias or error. These are often referred to as *cognitive distortions*. The list below outlines some of the more common cognitive errors or distortions and how they may appear in people who experience DPAFU. It's very unlikely that you have found yourself thinking all of these thoughts, or even most of them, but you've probably had a few of these thoughts at some time or another.

- **All or nothing thinking:** This is when things seem black or white with no in between. If it's not perfect then it's a failure; if it's not right then it must be wrong. *If my DPAFU is present then I won't enjoy the day*.
- **Negative mental filter:** You single out one negative detail and focus on it at the expense of any positive features. *You have a night out and focus on the brief period of time when you felt DPAFU. You then remember the whole evening as a disaster*.

- **Fortune-telling:** You predict the future as being negative. *My DPAFU will only get worse.*
- **Overgeneralization:** You make a whole pattern of negatives from just one or two instances. You did one thing wrong and think that you did everything wrong. *You blame all your negative sensations on DPAFU.*
- **Catastrophizing:** You view what has happened or what will happen as awful or unbearable. *My DPAFU will get worse, I will lose my job, my wife will leave me, I will be alone, I will lose my house etc.*
- **Labelling:** You use negative labels for yourself (and others) like *'I'm a failure'* or *'I'm useless'* or *'I'm mad'*.
- **Disqualifying the positive:** Even when you become aware of positives you find a way to discount them. *It's not that my DPAFU is better, it's that I don't notice it as much. I did enjoy the pub but my DPAFU spoilt it.*
- **Exaggeration:** You magnify any mistakes, mishaps or negatives. *You speak up at a meeting and don't believe you sounded as you hoped. Then you might think to yourself that everyone thought you were stupid and were laughing at you and you will probably lose your job. Or you think, if I go out when my DPAFU is bad everyone will know I've 'lost it' and my friends will abandon me.*
- **Jumping to conclusions:** You assume that you know what others think or feel about you or your behavior – you think you are an accurate *'mind reader'*. Or you think you know what will happen in the future, and that you are an accurate *'fortune teller'*. *If I go out when my DPAFU is bad everyone will know I feel strange and uncomfortable.*
- **Personalization:** If something bad happens you assume you are in some way responsible. *If something*

goes wrong at work then you assume it is just down to you and not in any way the department or system that is to blame.

- **Should statements:** These are the rules that you make for yourself. These rules tend to be inflexible and cause personal upset and distress when broken, often leading to feelings of guilt. *I should never had taken that drug or let stress get the better of me. If I hadn't then I would not be in this state (DPAFU) now.*

- **Emotional reasoning:** Assuming something to be true based on only a feeling. *I feel so odd this must be the first sign of madness.* This is one of the most common cognitive errors that people who suffer with DPAFU are prone to.

- **Blaming:** You focus on someone or something as the source of your negative feelings or problems. For example, *my DPAFU is to blame for my partner leaving. My DPAFU stops me from working.*

This is not an exhaustive list but it covers the most common cognitive errors reported by people with DPAFU.

Aaron T. Beck also observed that these cognitive distortions or errors were common to all people, whether or not they suffered from depression or other psychological problems. The distortions only became problematic when they occurred either too frequently, or when someone experienced a serious incident, such as a trauma or illness. In order to illustrate the different kind of automatic thoughts that might pop into your head in exactly the same situation, imagine you're walking down the street and you pass an old friend who does not acknowledge you – what is your first thought?

1 They did not see me.
2 They ignored me on purpose.
3 They never liked me.
4 They must have had things on their mind.

If you believed that numbers 1 or 4 were the case, you would probably feel only a slight or no emotional reaction. But if you believed numbers 2 or 3 to be true, you may be left feeling sad or angry. So how you interpret or understand a situation becomes very important in how you feel or experience emotion. If you believed numbers 1 or 4 to be the case, you may decide when you get home to give the person a call to see how they are. On the other hand, if you believed numbers 2 or 3 to be true, you may go home and think about why nobody likes you (even though you do not know this to be the case), or you may have an argument with a friend or partner.

These are all examples of how our mood or emotion affects how we behave. If you refer back to the list of common cognitive errors you will see that the errors for numbers 2 and 3 could be *jumping to conclusions, mind reading* or *fortune telling*. They could also be an example of a *negative mental filter* if you've previously had lots of positive experiences with the person you think is ignoring you. There are no right or wrong answers. A cognitive error or distortion may fall under the heading of more than one category. Indeed if everything always had to be either right or wrong then you may have fallen into the trap of *all or nothing thinking*, another cognitive error.

Cognitive behavioral therapy, or CBT, focuses on working with a person's thoughts, beliefs and interpretations (collectively known as *cognitions*), as well as changing their behavior patterns in order to have an effect upon their emotional problems. Cognitive therapy (CT), on the other hand, focuses primarily on cognitions by changing unhelpful thinking (although this will also have an impact on behavior patterns too, as you will learn later). We use the term CBT in this book to refer to both approaches. CBT is usually carried out by health care professionals such as clinical psychologists, nurses or counsellors who have undergone recognized training in this particular form of therapy. CBT has certain characteristics that distinguish it from other forms of talking therapies:

- CBT is relatively **short** in duration, usually lasting between 6 to 20 sessions.
- The focus is on the **'here-and-now'**. In other words, therapy does not dwell on past events but focuses on solving the problems you have right now.
- You work in **collaboration** with your therapist, forming a 'team' in which both of you are equal partners. Your therapist will be knowledgeable about CBT but you are the expert on you!
- CBT is **educational** and aims to teach you **skills** that will enable you to eventually become your own therapist.
- In CBT you take an **active** approach to solving your own problems. Therapy is not something that is 'done' to you.
- It is based on **scientific principles**, and you are like a scientist testing out theories and hypotheses based on your thoughts and behaviors.

How does CBT work?

At the end of Part 1 you identified and listed ways in which your DPAFU affected you on five different levels:

1 **Cognitive:** thoughts, beliefs, meanings images, attention and memory.
2 **Emotional:** how you feel, your moods, numbness.
3 **Behavioral:** what you do more or less of, things you avoid.
4 **Physical:** bodily changes, sleep patterns, numbness.
5 **Environmental:** situations, relationships, work, home.

The psychological model given in the last chapter included these five systems. Two American therapists who are experts in CBT, Drs Padesky and Greenberger, have incorporated these different systems into their Five Systems model, which has proved very helpful for CBT. Figure 5.1 illustrates how this works.

The idea is that at any given moment these five systems are all interacting with each other. The four systems of cognition, emotion, behavior and physical sensations are

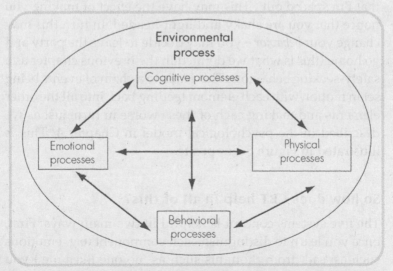

Figure 5.1   The Five Systems Model – Greenberger & Padesky (1995)

linked to each other. In addition, each of these four systems also interacts with the outside environment (shown in the diagram within a circle). If you look at Figure 5.1, you will see that the arrows between each of the systems are double-ended. This is because each of the systems has an impact on each other in both directions. For example, your thoughts or cognitions can affect your behavior, but so too can your behavior affect your thoughts, and so on.

As we have already identified, DPAFU affects each of these five systems, and so a therapeutic approach that includes each of these systems is likely to be helpful. CBT therapy follows this approach and is focused on identifying and understanding your problems and how they affect your mood, thoughts and behavior in day-to-day life. The relationship between your moods, thoughts and behaviors is then explored and the impact one has upon the other is revealed. For example, imagine you are in a busy social situation, such as a party, and your DPAFU worsens. You might think: 'Everyone will notice that I'm spaced out'. This may have the effect of making you notice that you are shaky and light-headed. In turn this may change your *behavior* – you may decide to leave the party and go home (this is what we defined in the previous chapter as a safety-seeking behavior). This leads to a chain of events being set in motion with each element feeding back into all the other elements and making each of these worse in turn, just as we described in the psychological model in Chapter 4. This is illustrated in Figure 5.2 opposite.

So how does CBT help in all of this?

The five systems concept is helpful in two main ways. First, once you learn to distinguish each component (e.g. emotions such as 'sad' from thoughts such as 'no one likes me') you can start to understand what is happening to you. This

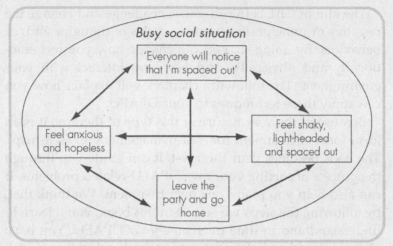

Figure 5.2 Example using the Five Systems Model – Greenberger & Padesky (1995)

understanding will make your experience seem less overwhelming and confusing. Second, if all five systems are interacting with each other, changing one of the interacting systems will cause a change in all the other components. For example, just by changing your thoughts you can have an effect on your emotions, your physical sensations, your behavior and how you interact with the environment.

Using the example given in Figure 5.2 above, think about what would happen if you were able to replace the unhelpful thought 'everyone will notice that I'm spaced out', with a more helpful thought such as 'even though I am experiencing some sensations of DPAFU I know that this is not noticeable to other people'. How would this affect how you feel? Do you think you would feel less anxious and hopeless? Do you think that your physical sensations might improve? Do you think you might be able to stay at the party instead of giving up and going home? Do you think that you might interact differently with people at the party?

The aim of CBT is to recognize, challenge and change the negative or unhelpful patterns or cycles of thoughts and/or behaviors. By doing so, you can change how you feel emotionally and physically, and how you interact with your environment. The following chapters will explain how you can apply these techniques to your DPAFU.

Because of the very nature of this type of therapy, it is an ideal form of treatment for 'self-management' or 'self-help'. The book becomes your therapist. It can guide you through the process of solving your own DPAFU-related problems. It can also help you plan your own treatment. We think that, by following the steps we set out in this book, you'll learn to understand and in time overcome your DPAFU. You have already completed the first two steps by deciding which DPAFU sensations are relevant to you, and thinking about how often they occur (see the sensation checklist on page 6). The second exercise at the end of Chapter 4 (page 37) got you thinking about the impact of DPAFU on the systems that make up the Five Systems model.

However, if after reading through this book and trying out the exercises for yourself, you feel that you need more than a self-help guide to CBT, your GP will probably be the best person to approach. Your GP can refer you to a therapist who works within the NHS. This treatment will be free. Alternatively, you could opt for private treatment, which costs on average between £50 and £80 per session (usually about an hour). CBT is usually carried out by health care professionals such as clinical psychologists, nurses or counsellors who have undergone recognized training in this particular form of therapy. The British Association for Behavioural and Cognitive Psychotherapies (BABCP) or the British Psychological Society (BPS) will be able to provide you with the name of an accredited therapist in your local area (see the section on Further Information for useful addresses). You do need to be aware that DPAFU is only now being recognized as relatively common and open to some CBT approaches. Even some psychiatrists are not aware of the condition and would say they have not seen many cases. As we have mentioned, DPAFU has not accrued the large body of research evidence for treatment with CBT that has been developed for depression, panic attacks, phobias, obsessive compulsive disorder and so on. In fact that is the main reason we wrote this book! You may find that if you take the book along with you when you see a therapist or doctor it will help them learn more about the problem and direct them towards more information.

6

Dealing with the core problem

Defining the problem

Distinguishing DPAFU from other problems

The first step in the process of CBT is being able to identify exactly what the problem is. Until you've defined a problem accurately it's difficult to know when it is getting better (or worse). Saying how you feel is only a starting point, because this is a reflection of your thoughts, moods and behaviors and so is liable to biases (or your interpretations as discussed in Chapter 4). For example, simply saying that you *feel unwell* is very vague. You get a more useful definition when you think of feeling unwell in terms of its component parts, for example having a sore throat, a headache and a temperature. To make the definition of unwell even more useful, you can use numbers to measure each of these parts, e.g. having a sore throat. Allocate a number to the soreness on a scale of 0–10, with 0 representing no soreness or pain at all and 10 being extremely sore. If you score 7 on day one and 5 on day two a reduction of 2 points shows improvement. In the same way, an increase in scores from say 7 to 9 indicates more soreness.

The same rules can be applied to DPAFU. Firstly you need to *identify* all the different *sensations* associated with DPAFU. Secondly, you need to create a way to *measure the intensity or severity* of these sensations. This will help you see whether they are getting worse, staying the same, or improving. You can then assess the *impact* that DPAFU is having on your life. For example, is it making you do more, or less, of particular activities? We'll show you how to apply these techniques later in this chapter.

Before you can progress with the management of your DPAFU, you need to be clear about the impact DPAFU has on your life. It's natural to have days when you feel low, exhausted or detached. This happens to everyone. But it can be unhelpful and inaccurate to attribute all your negative sensations and experiences to DPAFU. At the Unit in London we carried out research that looked at the types of sensations people with DPAFU associate with their condition. From our research we know that people believe that a wide range of experiences come under the DPAFU heading. These include the expected sensations, such as feeling unreal, seeing the world through a veil or pane of glass and a loss of a sense of self. But we also found that people associated more general sensations, such as loss of pleasure, poor concentration and breathlessness, with their DPAFU. These general sensations could equally be associated with something else, such as anxiety, stress or depression.

So how do you separate the sensations produced by DPAFU from your feelings of anxiety, stress or depression? Doing this can be difficult, but completing the checklist on the following pages can help. There is some blank space for you to add in any of your own. Once you've completed the list think about whether or not you think these sensations relate to your DPAFU or to something else. Do keep in mind the following questions:

- How do I feel when I am stressed and/or anxious?
- How do I feel when I feel low or depressed?
- How are these feelings different from DPAFU?
- Can I separate out my feelings or do I see them as all being part of one condition?

You may be wondering why it's so important to look carefully at your sensations and how you feel. Have a look back at the model we set out in Chapter 4 (see page 35). If you assume that any negative sensation is part of the DPAFU, then it will seem like the DPAFU is getting worse which will naturally lead to more anxiety or worry. As we know, anxiety and worry bring with them different sensations in their own right, both physical and emotional. You may then be aware of more sensations, or sensations of greater intensity, and think that they're a part of DPAFU. This will in turn confirm your belief that the DPAFU is getting worse! You're caught up in a negative cycle. You can break negative cycles, but you have to recognize them first.

Listed on pages 56–57 are a number of sensations that you may have experienced since your DPAFU began. Read the instructions at the top of each column carefully. They ask you different questions in relation to your sensations.

Measuring the intensity of your DPAFU

Next, to help you monitor your progress, you need to rate the intensity or severity of each of your sensations of DPAFU on a scale of 0–10. Zero represents the negative, i.e. the worst the sensation could ever be, and the top score of 10 represents the positive, i.e. the best the sensation could ever be. For example, for the sensation of 'feeling emotionally numb', a score of 0 would mean that you are feeling nothing at all, and a score of 10 would mean that you are feeling your emotions to the fullest. You then need to think about what a score of 5 or 6 might feel like. Many people who report that they feel emotionally numb often find they do actually feel something, but those feelings are negative ones, like anger, frustration and fear. A common mistake is to believe that because you don't feel any positive emotions, then you're not feeling anything. Bear this in mind when you complete your diary and make sure that when you give a score of 0 you really do have a complete absence of feeling at all times.

What next? Once you have a firm idea of what a score of 0, 5 and 10 represent, you can begin to fill in all the numbers in between. This will make monitoring change much easier (see the example in Table 6.1 on page 60). You should also then decide which number you would be happy with. It may not be realistic to always aim for number 10!

It's very important that you focus on *one* sensation (or the absence of that sensation) at a time. A blank table is included on page 61 for you to copy and complete for each of the sensations that you experience. You'll find another blank copy in Appendix III. Table 6.1 on page 60 provides examples for the DPAFU sensation of 'feeling emotionally numb'. Try to include both positive and negative feelings. For example, you may believe that because you do not feel happiness, love and joy, or you do not feel connected to other people, then you must be feeling nothing. But the feelings of frustration and irritation that you felt while you were at work also count. They may not be the emotional feelings you want, but they are still feelings.

You could use this example for yourself, but it's best if you make it more personal and specific to you. You can do this by defining the feelings *you* actually experience.

Checklist to identify sensations related to DPAFU and those related to other factors. For the first two columns, tick which sensations apply to you.

	Have you experienced this sensation since your DPAFU began?	This sensation is related to my DPAFU	This sensation is related to other factors (please list)
Visual disturbance			
Feelings of unreality			
Lack of spontaneity			
Breathlessness			
Increased worry			
Emotional numbing			
Fatigue			
Shakiness/dizziness			
World appears 2D			
Loss of pleasure			

Seeing the world through a veil/glass	Depressed mood	Loss of a sense of self	Light sensitivity or flashes	Restlessness	Feeling like a robot	Pounding heart	Irritability	Headaches	Panic attacks	Sleep difficulties	Poor sense of time	Unable to feel stress	Poor concentration or memory

Please list below any sensations not already listed that you believe are part of your experience of DPAFU.

If 0 is the worst the sensation could be and 10 is the best, think about what each of the points in between would be like. Fill these in on Table 6.2 on page 61. Think about the sensations you experience. On a scale of 0–10 how do you rate their severity?

Assessing the impact DPAFU has on your life

Now you are able to think about the problematic sensations associated with DPAFU and you've given a numerical value to each to help you measure change. Next you need to think about what your sensations of DPAFU either prevent you from doing or make you do. How do these sensations interfere with your ability to function the way you would like to? What impact do they have on how you think or how you do things? Answering these questions will help you build a realistic picture of the impact the sensations have upon your life. Again, you need to be *specific* when answering these questions. Instead of simply stating that they make you 'feel unreal' and that you don't enjoy life to the full, try to get a clear picture of all the sensations you experience, and the impact they have on your life. So think about the activities these sensations stop you from doing, those you avoid and/or those you increase. Once you have a clear picture you can begin to see exactly what you'd like to change.

For example, if you are feeling 'unreal' you might decide you don't want to go out. Perhaps this is because you believe that other people will see just how 'odd' you are. So you don't go out. But this means you never get to find out if this belief about how other people see you is true or not. You also miss out on any fun. As a result, you may feel that your 'quality of life' is poor. One way to overcome the problem is to start going out again. While it may not directly help you 'feel real', it will certainly give you a sense of pleasure, and

TABLE 6.1: MEASURING THE INTENSITY OF DPAFU: AN EXAMPLE

Numerical value	PROBLEMATIC SENSATION *Feeling emotionally numb*
0	I feel nothing. I never laugh or cry. I feel emotion for 0 minutes on 0 days of the week. I have no emotions.
1	Momentary feeling(s) lasting 0–5 minutes one day per week.
2	Momentary feeling(s) lasting 0–5 minutes 2–5 days per week.
3	Awareness of some emotional feeling(s) lasting 5–30 minutes one day per week.
4	Awareness of some emotional feeling(s) lasting 5–30 minutes 2–5 days per week.
5	Being aware of some emotional feelings (negative or positive) for one hour or more per day for at least two days per week.
6	Being aware of some emotional feelings (negative or positive) for one hour or more per day for at least five days per week.
7	Being able to identify at least two different mood states at least five days per week but without being consciously aware of them.
8	Being able to identify 3–5 different mood states every day.
9	I am aware that I feel a wide variety of emotions everyday, but I do not focus on how I feel.
10	I feel happy, sad, anxious, frustrated, contented, worried, stressed. I am able to express how I feel. I am not aware of it – I just do it.

Numerical value	PROBLEMATIC SENSATION
TABLE 6.2: MEASURING THE INTENSITY OF DPAFU: BLANK SHEET	
0	
1	
2	
3	
4	
5	
6	
7	
8	
9	
10	

TABLE 6.3: MINA'S EXAMPLE

Sensation	Makes you do more	Makes you do less
Visual – it feels like I see the world through a pane of glass.	Check my eyesight. Check whether I'm seeing things oddly in other ways.	Drive – I am frightened I will have/cause an accident, especially on the motorway.
Numbness – I don't feel any emotions at all.	Check for any signs of emotion. Try to figure out why I feel this way.	Spend time with my partner/family as I feel guilty that I do not feel love for them – even though I know in my head I do.
I don't recognize myself when I look in the mirror.	Check to see if it's still happening.	Avoid looking at reflections of myself because I don't want to be reminded of how weird I feel.

you will be able to test out your belief that other people see you as 'odd'. You'll also feel a sense of accomplishment. It may make you feel that you have some control over DPAFU, rather than DPAFU controlling you.

Next, have a look at the example opposite from Mina (Table 6.3). This will give you some idea of how you can begin to think more specifically about your behaviors. Once you've established a profile of your problems, you can begin to question yourself i.e. 'to what extent is it really a problem?' Again, there's a blank table on page 66 for you to copy and complete with your own answers, and another blank copy in Appendix III.

The first example Mina mentions – *feeling as if I see the world through a pane of glass* (or a goldfish bowl, piece of cloth, thick mist etc.) – can become *more* of a problem if we behave in certain ways. For example, if you pay close attention to how you are seeing things, and check your eyesight frequently, you'll become more aware of the problem. This is simply because you are thinking about it more. This focusing on a sensation, and constant checking to see how it's affecting you, can easily lead to that sensation continuing, as we saw on pages 32–33.

Mina's concerns about her eyesight lead to her driving less, since she is worried that she may cause an accident. She may begin to take the bus instead to go about her day-to-day business and, as a result, the visual disturbance may become less of a problem in the short term. But once you begin to drive less and actively avoid doing so, a new problem is formed – one of *avoidance*. It may get to the point that you feel you are no longer able to drive. In fact, you may end up believing that you'd cause an accident if you did drive. But remember: because you're not driving you can't prove this belief to be wrong. Avoidance can make you feel that you're less able to do the things you used to be able to do. This in turn can lower your mood and lead you to worry that your sensations of DPAFU are getting worse. This can then lead to another negative cycle. Happily, CBT is extremely effective at dealing with avoidance.

Mina also mentions *emotional numbness*, and this can also become more of a problem as a result of certain behavior. Avoiding contact with people, or constantly checking for numbness, can perpetuate the feeling of 'disconnectedness' and lead to the problem continuing. Keeping an accurate diary for a week or two of how exactly you are feeling is likely to show some emotional variation, although those emotions might be negative. You might, for example, say that you feel nothing at all and that nothing either bothers or excites you. After keeping a diary as described on page 71, you'll realize that there *was* emotional variation within your week. Perhaps you felt stressed at work when asked to do something and/or frustrated that your DPAFU was not getting better. Either way, stress and/or frustration are emotions – they just happen not to be pleasant ones.

Mina's final example of *failing to recognize herself* becomes more of a problem if you begin to change your behavior in particular ways. (You might want to have a look back at Jay's case on page 15 to see how this feeling affected him.) Frequently checking yourself in the mirror may reinforce your symptoms of DPAFU. For instance, if every time you look at yourself you are reminded that you don't recognize the reflection, and you do this 30 times a day, then 30 times a day you are reinforcing the feeling of not recognizing yourself. Try to only look in the mirror for a specific purpose, for example to apply make-up, do your hair or have a shave. Don't look to check if you are 'you' or to see whether the way you feel has changed.

Alternatively, you might actively avoid looking in the mirror because you find it distressing. Like all types of avoidance, you'll find yourself avoiding more and more situations, such as seeing your reflection in shop windows or in shiny objects. Some people even avoid looking at cutlery in case they see their reflection. If you find yourself avoiding looking at your reflection, you should begin to use the mirror on a daily basis for a specific purpose, but not to check or validate how you feel about yourself. Whether you check your reflection repeatedly, or avoid it completely, you can end up being distanced from yourself. You become like an outside observer or you lose spontaneity and become self-conscious. Both being completely detached from your emotions or going to the opposite extreme and being totally swayed by your feelings from moment to moment at the expense of other evidence can become problems in their own right. Incidentally, having your thoughts overly influenced by your feelings is sometimes called *emotional reasoning*. We look at emotional reasoning, and other common cognitive errors, on pages 42–44.

With human nature being what it is, it's not surprising that you would want to check to see if the DPAFU is getting better or worse. As we've mentioned, one way to do this might be by checking your reflection in the mirror. But if you look in the mirror and find that the way you feel hasn't changed, it will reinforce the feelings associated with DPAFU. This behavior then helps continue the problem, leading to another cycle of checking and so on.

If you've found the previous paragraphs difficult to follow, it might be worth going back to the first part of the book and re-reading the psychological causes of DPAFU (pages 27–35). Be sure that you have identified the sensations you associate with DPAFU – you can do this by completing the checklist on pages 56–57. Identify those sensations that are having a significant impact on your everyday life by completing Table 6.2 on page 61. Once you have identified the key points you can see how your experiences fit within the model we set out on page 35.

Now think about the sensations you experience and the impact they have on your behavior. What do you find yourself repeating or doing more of? What do you avoid or do less of?

Setting goals

If you can really define your DPAFU sensations, it'll help you manage them more effectively. You'll also need to think about how you'll know when you feel better and when things have changed. Although this sounds obvious, it's very important to identify 'benchmarks' that show how things have changed for you. Often people say that their goal for self-help or treatment is simply to 'feel better'. But this is very vague and it doesn't fully explain what it means to feel better. So, you need to be as specific as possible, for example

TABLE 6.4: RECORDING SPECIFIC SENSATIONS AND BEHAVIORS: BLANK SHEET		
Sensation	Makes you do more	Makes you do less

'I would like to feel less cut off from things or to feel more real'.

Next you need to consider exactly how you'll know when this has happened. How will you know when you are feeling 'real'? It's tempting to believe you'll just know, but you have to be wary of relying on *emotional reasoning* (see page 44). And, if you don't pinpoint as exactly as possible what it means to feel real, you may find that you've set yourself an unrealistic goal. Think about these sorts of questions: 'How will others know I am better?'; 'What will be different when I feel better?'; 'What will I be able to do?'; 'What will I stop doing?'. Because answers to these questions are not always obvious or easy to identify, it's a good idea to keep a diary over a couple of weeks to help you record your thoughts, feelings, actions, and interpretations. You may want to write your diary when your DPAFU feels particularly intense. Or, if your DPAFU is constant, you may decide to complete the diary at the same time each day, such as in the evening.

By now you should have made a list of each of the problematic sensations you associate with DPAFU. You have learned to rate the different sensations of your DPAFU on a scale of 0–10. You should have also considered the activities DPAFU prevents you from doing and those that it causes you to increase. Once the problem is well-defined, setting the goal for what you would like to achieve with this book is much easier.

Try to make your goals as SMART as possible:

- Specific (*so you know exactly what the goal is*).
- Measurable (*so you can measure change*).
- Achievable (*so you don't set yourself up to fail*).
- Realistic (*so that it is within your capabilities or possibilities*).
- Time limited (*so that it does not go on indefinitely*).

When you break a problem down into smaller units things appear more manageable. Keeping records of how you feel early on in the process also provides you with the evidence of how things are changing for you over time.

On a scale of 0–10 rate where you are now and where you would like to be. Where you would like to be will become part of your *goals*. You can devise your own scale, but be sure to use the same scale throughout these exercises. It is common to use low numbers to denote negatives and high numbers to reflect positives. Don't automatically go for 10 as your final goal. Instead try to be realistic, and settle on a number that would be 'good enough'. Think about how much of an issue the specific problem actually is for you. Sometimes we have to learn to accept experiences or sensations that we would rather not have, and so we 'manage' rather than 'cure' them. Think too about the impact the sensations or symptoms associated with DPAFU have on your everyday life. Identify those activities that you would like to do more of and those you would like to stop avoiding.

So using the blank table opposite (Table 6.6) fill out each box as it applies to you. We've included a completed example (Table 6.5) to help you think about the way in which you can complete the boxes. The object of this exercise is to define each of the components that make up DPAFU for you and see how they impact upon your life currently. Next you need to consider your target or goal for change. Defining each component of the overall problem allows you to decide which aspect you would like to work on first. As the saying goes, a journey of a thousand miles begins with one step.

Here's an example of how the completed boxes may look. Remember there are no right or wrong answers. The aim of

TABLE 6.5: EXAMPLE OF GOAL-SETTING SHEET

Problematic sensation Current score 0–10 Target score 0–10	Increased activities	Decreased activities
I feel emotionally numb 2/10. My target is 7/10.	I often pinch myself to see if I can feel. I often check out if I am actually feeling anything when I know I should.	I tend to spend less time around people as I feel disconnected from them and this only leaves me feeling worse.
I feel unreal 0/10. My target score is 8/10.	I check myself in the mirror to see if I can feel 'me'. I try to figure it out by thinking about things.	I don't go out so much as I often feel worse outside. If I am having a bad episode I lie down in the dark. I can't watch TV as this makes it worse.

TABLE 6.6: BLANK GOAL-SETTING SHEET

Problematic sensation Current score 0–10 Target score 0–10	Increased activities	Decreased activities

this exercise is to help you to identify areas that you wish to change.

When you fill in the boxes, it'll become clear that there are things you can begin to change. Using Table 6.5, one of the goals might be to stop pinching yourself irrespective of how you are feeling. This doesn't provide proof of who you are, but instead reinforces your belief that something is wrong. Usually the activities you increase or avoid because of the DPAFU will also help the DPAFU feelings continue. Goals such as stopping pinching yourself are a starting point, but they can still be made SMARTer.

Here are some of the most common reasons for finding these exercises difficult:

- Goals are far too big and unrealistic.
- Goals are not specific enough. For instance, a goal to go out more needs to be more clearly defined. It's best to be as specific as possible, i.e. go out twice a week for two hours, once to the pub and once to the cinema.
- There is no form of measurement at the beginning from which to monitor change.
- Goals are too easy to achieve and so aren't a challenge.
- There's no time frame, which can sometimes lead to a feeling of drifting along so you may lose a sense of direction. This can in turn reduce your motivation and self-discipline.

Before we move on to the next section, have a think about the following question: *when is a problem not a problem?* The answer is: when you say so! People vary in the ways they perceive problems in life. If you feel 'a bit odd' but still go to work, and then go out with friends in the evening, then feeling a bit odd does not stop you from leading a normal day-to-day life. In this instance, feeling odd is not a problem. But if when you feel a bit odd you take the day off work, stay in bed and worry about the way you feel, it becomes a problem. This is especially so if it happens often, or if you believe the odd feeling is the result of something you've done (like take a drug), or if it appeared to come out of the blue and you spent time trying to figure out why it happened. In each of these situations, you would begin to experience the sensations as problematic. It's always worth having another think about each of the sensations you've defined as being problematic. At this stage you may want to redefine the different levels at which DPAFU affects you, what exactly each problem stops you from doing, and how it operates.

Diary keeping

Keeping a diary of your DPAFU sensations can be very helpful for several reasons:

- It can give an accurate measurement of the frequency and intensity of your DPAFU as it stands now. After you've tried out the techniques we describe in the following sections of the book, you can keep another diary. Then you can compare them to see how your sensations of DPAFU have changed and in what ways.
- Rating the intensity of your DPAFU sensations at frequent intervals can help you identify whether there are any fluctuations.

- Noting down your thoughts, emotions and current environment can help show any patterns accompanying your DPAFU. This will help you see patterns of which you may have been previously unaware.
- Gaining a better understanding of what affects your DPAFU will give you a greater sense of control. This is because it will enable you to try to decrease the situations that cause your DPAFU to worsen and increase the situations that improve it.

Before we go on, a word of caution. Keeping a diary of this kind is a staple of CBT treatment for a number of conditions, especially anxiety and depression, and has been used by probably thousands if not millions of people over the years. We think it can help many people with DPAFU. However, DPAFU can take different forms and, as you'd expect, people can react to it in different ways. So some people may not find keeping a diary beneficial. One of the patterns of thinking and behavior that we have observed in our depersonalization clinic is that it is easy for people to get caught up in observing themselves and their actions – not to find ways of breaking cycles of behavior, but rather as a way of proving to themselves that they really are experiencing DPAFU. It becomes a self-fulfilling prophecy. For example, you might say to yourself: 'I bet when I go to work tomorrow I will be mechanical and unspontaneous, not like a real person'. You then spend all your energies analysing a minute gesture made by a colleague or a chance remark made by a friend for 'evidence' that they think you're not behaving normally. You then devote far too long to recording tiny instances when maybe you could have reacted differently. If this is what you do, you need to change your approach.

With these cautions in mind, there are two types of diary

we recommend. The first is a diary in which you rate the severity of your DPAFU on an hourly basis. This is useful if your DPAFU is constant and/or appears to lack any variation. The second type of diary is one in which you record the situations, thoughts, emotions, behaviors and sensations that accompany your DPAFU. This type of diary is best if you experience DPAFU intermittently.

The hourly diary for continual DPAFU

People who suffer with continual DPAFU frequently report no variation at all in how they feel. Their sensations seem constant and unremitting. However, after closer examination, it is often found that there are very slight and subtle variations in the DPAFU sensations. These may be difficult to recognize at first.

Table 6.7 on pages 76–78 presents an example of a partly completed diary to show you how it might look when it is completed. Table 6.8 on pages 80–81 is a blank hourly diary for you to complete. You'll find another blank copy in Appendix III. You will see that the diary looks rather like a timetable, with the days along the top and the time (in hours) down the side. For each hour, briefly describe the situation you are in and then rate the intensity of your DPAFU, from 0 (indicating none whatsoever) to 10 (indicating the worst your DPAFU has ever been). There are no right or wrong responses to this – just note down whatever score seems most appropriate to describe how you are feeling.

Alexi's partly completed diary is on pages 76–78.

If we look at Alexi's diary we can see that, although he experiences DPAFU all the time, the intensity of this varies quite significantly depending on his situation. Using the detailed information from the diary we can see the times when his DPAFU is at the lowest and highest points and see if any patterns emerge. One way of doing this is to categorize his activities according to their DPAFU scores:

High DPAFU activities (scores from 8–10)

- Meeting with boss
- Shopping in supermarket
- Travelling to work (when busy)
- Presentation to clients
- Talking to clients
- Talking to new people (in social situation)
- Meeting Liz for meal
- Driving

Moderate DPAFU activities (scores from 4–7)

- Travelling to/from work
- Paperwork at work
- Phone calls at work
- Preparing presentation
- Meeting at work
- Meeting friends for a drink in a bar
- Shopping and lunch in town
- Chatting in the club house
- Watching film with Liz
- Drinking in pub with Liz

Low DPAFU activities (scores from 0–3)

- Meals at home
- Lunch in the park
- Watching TV
- Reading in bed
- Showering
- Chatting to best friend/father
- Doing housework
- Playing football
- Listening to the radio
- Lunch with family

Review of Alexi's Diary

Alexi's DPAFU sensations appear to be at their worst in stressful work and social situations. This is especially when he has to interact with new people, lots of people or people who increase his anxiety (such as his boss or having a meal with Liz). Crowded and brightly lit environmental situations, such as travelling and supermarket shopping, also increase his DPAFU. Alexi's DPAFU sensations worsen when he has to drive. However, when he is at work and in social situations where he feels more comfortable, his DPAFU is lower. The lowest levels are when he is quiet at home, experiencing physical sensations such as showering or playing football, or when he is with close family and friends.

Try to keep your own hourly diary for a week – but no longer than that. Next, look to see what patterns emerge. If you fill in the DPAFU rating as soon as possible, rather than leave it till the end of the day, it will be more accurate. If you forget about the diary for a time, don't worry. Just start again and fill it in when you remember. It's better if the information is accurate but patchy than if you complete it in

TABLE 6.7: EXAMPLE OF AN HOURLY DPAFU DIARY: ALEXI

Time	Monday	Tuesday	Wednesday	Thursday	Friday	Saturday	Sunday
6–7 a.m.				Sleep	Sleep	Sleep	Sleep
7–8 a.m.				Breakfast DP 2	Breakfast DP 3	Sleep	Sleep
8–9 a.m.				Travel to work DP 6	Travel to work (busy) DP 8	Breakfast DP 1	Sleep
9–10 a.m.				Paperwork DP 5	Presentation to clients DP 10	Tidy flat DP 2	Read papers DP 1
10–11 a.m.				Meeting with boss DP 9	Talk to clients DP 9	Go shopping in town DP 4	Listen to radio DP 1
11–12 p.m.				Meeting with boss DP 8	Finish meeting DP 6	Go shopping in town DP 4	Tidy up DP 1

Time				
12–1 p.m.	Drive to parents DP 8	Lunch in town DP 4	Write report DP 5	Phone calls DP 6
1–2 p.m.	Help prepare lunch DP 2	Get kit together DP 3	Lunch with friend DP 4	Lunch in park DP 3
2–3 p.m.	Lunch with family DP 3	Football in park DP 2	Phone calls DP 5	Prepare presentation DP 5
3–4 p.m.	Chat to Dad DP 2	Football DP 2	Paperwork DP 4	Prepare presentation DP 6
4–5 p.m.	Drive home DP 8	Shower DP 1	Plan for next week DP 4	Phone calls DP 5
5–6 p.m.		In the club house DP 4	Travel home DP 5	Travel home DP 6
6–7 p.m.		Go home/change DP 3	Shower DP 2	Shop in supermarket DP 8

TABLE 6.7: EXAMPLE OF AN HOURLY DPAFU DIARY: ALEXI (cont.)

Time	Monday	Tuesday	Wednesday	Thursday	Friday	Saturday	Sunday
7–8 p.m.				Eat meal DP 3	Meet friends for drinks in bar DP 5	Meet Liz for meal DP 8	
8–9 p.m.				Watch TV DP 3	Chat with best friend DP 3	Watch film DP 5	
9–10 p.m.				Watch TV DP 1	Talk to new people DP 8	Watch film DP 4	
10–11 p.m.				Read in bed DP1	Go home DP 4	Drink in pub DP 7	
11–12 a.m.				Sleep	Sleep	Home – watch TV DP 3	
12–1 a.m.				Sleep	Sleep	Sleep	

retrospect by trying to remember how you felt at the time. If the week you chose to keep the diary turns out to be very untypical of your normal pattern, then it may be advisable to try again another week. The longer you complete the diary, the more information you'll get, but generally a week or two is enough for clear patterns to emerge.

The STEBS diary for intermittent DPAFU

If your DPAFU is intermittent and comes and goes at different times, you might want to complete a diary that records your situations (S), thoughts (T), emotions (E), behavior (B) and sensations (S) (or *STEBS*) in order to detect any patterns that may be affecting your sensations. One suggestion is to think back over the day, identify the best and worst bits, and then record what you were doing at these times. What were your thoughts at these times? How did you actually feel and what did you do? This will help you notice any variations. You may find this difficult at first, because it may feel like there are no best or worst bits. However, you may notice times when you expected to feel something but did not, and vice versa. Try to be specific when you describe how you were feeling. For example, instead of saying you felt 'upset', see if you can distinguish whether you were sad, frustrated or anxious. Similarly, try to be as precise as you can if you feel cut off from your emotions. Instead of stating that you felt 'nothing', perhaps you can pin down whether you felt detached, numb, blank or spaced out.

Overleaf is a sample diary. There's no set format to this type of diary so we suggest you try something similar to the example provided and then adapt it to meet your needs. The essential components are to record how you're feeling physically and emotionally. Also record the thoughts associated with these feelings and what you were doing before, during

TABLE 6.8: HOURLY DPAFU DIARY

Rate your DPAFU every hour using the scale below:

0 — 1 — 2 — 3 — 4 — 5 — 6 — 7 — 8 — 9 — 10

No DPAFU at all   Moderate DPAFU   Worst DPAFU

Time	Monday	Tuesday	Wednesday	Thursday	Friday	Saturday	Sunday
6–7 a.m.							
7–8 a.m.							
8–9 a.m.							
9–10 a.m.							
10–11 a.m.							
11–12 p.m.							
12–1 p.m.							
1–2 p.m.							

2–3 p.m.	3–4 p.m.	4–5 p.m.	5–6 p.m.	6–7 p.m.	7–8 p.m.	8–9 p.m.	9–10 p.m.	10–11 p.m.	11–12 a.m.	12–1 a.m.

TABLE 6.9: EXAMPLE OF A STEBS DIARY FOR INTERMITTANT DPAFU

Situation	Thoughts	Emotion	Behaviors	Sensations
Sitting watching TV.	It looks unreal. What is wrong with me?	Worried	Stop watching TV and check my vis on every 5 minutes.	Floaters are getting worse.
Driving in my car.	What happens if that weird visual thing happens? I will crash the car and I will kill somebody.	Anxious	I get home as quickly as I can. I have decided to only drive short journeys from now on, just in case.	My heart rate has gone up. I'm feeling panicky.
Sitting on the sofa just before bed.	Why can't I feel anything?	Frustrated	Go to bed and lie awake trying to figure things out.	I am emotionally numb.

TABLE 6.10: STEBS DIARY

Situation	Thoughts	Emotion	Behaviors	Sensations

and after these thoughts. We have included a blank diary sheet for you to copy on page 83 and in Appendix III.

Once you have kept a diary for a week or two you will begin to get a clearer picture of how DPAFU is affecting you. This will provide a good basis for you to really pinpoint how the sensations associated with DPAFU impact upon your life. At this point, we recommend that you look over the list you made at the end of Chapter 4 of how DPAFU affects you on different levels. You can now add to or amend this list.

One word of caution: our research has found that it is very common to notice an increase in DPAFU sensations when you first begin to talk or think about them more. Again this ties in with the model outlined in Chapter 4. The more you think about symptoms or sensations, the more you look for them and monitor them, and so the more you notice. The more you notice, the more you think about them, look for them and monitor them. However, this initial stage is an important part of self-managing your DPAFU.

Diary keeping is a powerful tool. Use it for a specific purpose – e.g. 'I want to see if my sensations differ according to the time of day' – not as an open-ended habit or substitute for living. Restrict diary keeping to the sort of formats recommended above and don't make it a repository of how bad you feel and all that is wrong with the world. If you're worried about becoming obsessed with observing yourself, or if you've recognized that this is a problem you would like to avoid, restrict yourself to a set period of updating and review – say half an hour in the evening.

Building an explanation that fits

The diary and problem definition exercises are designed to help you to identify the sensations associated with your DPAFU, to rate the intensity of these sensations, and to

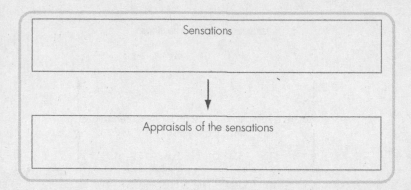

understand the impact they are having on your life. Now you have done this you can begin to identify your thoughts about these sensations to see how they affect your behavior. All of this information can then be fitted into the psychological model we outlined in the first part of the book. To begin with, consider the sensations you experience and the sense you make of them. This is what we are referring to when we talk about 'appraisals' or 'interpretations'. Use the boxes above to write down the main sensations of DPAFU that you experience. Then consider what these sensations lead you to think.

Once you've done this, you can begin to build up a picture of how these appraisals affect your mood. You will need to identify the ways in which you notice your symptoms, and how, when and where you become aware of them. Next you need to think about how all this affects your mood and emotions. Again, use the empty boxes overleaf.

Finally, try to identify your *safety-seeking behaviors*. These are the things you do (sayings, behaviors, rituals, thoughts) or avoid (situations, activities, people or places). These behaviors may make you feel that the DPAFU is more manageable, or help you cope or to feel better. In the first box are some examples. Use the second box to identify your own.

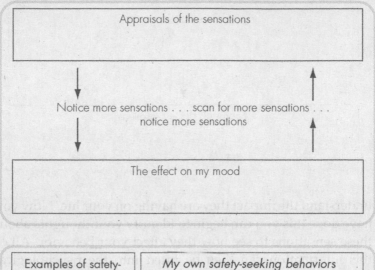

Once you've completed this basic model, you'll have a clearer idea of some of the things that lead to the problem continuing. You can then decide where to begin to tackle the problem. *Always remember to break things down into more manageable chunks. Take one step at a time so that you do not feel overwhelmed by your problems*. It is often advisable to begin with a smaller or less significant problem until you've got the hang of the techniques outlined in this book. If you try to focus on all of your problems, you can easily feel overwhelmed or disheartened.

You may be thinking that none of this applies to you. You may feel that the type of DPAFU you suffer with is more about 'emotional detachment' or 'numbness' and that there are actually no variations and no emotions. Even so, you'll probably still experience this numbness as distressing and as something sinister or worrying. Otherwise you wouldn't see yourself as having a problem and wouldn't need to consult a self-help book. So what you see as a lack or absence of emotion is a problem and it can be treated in the same way as the issues we've just described. And in fact the distress, upset or sadness that the numbness brings *are* actually emotions. On the other hand, if you're truly not bothered by feeling nothing or numbness, then it's not a problem.

Perhaps you're not consciously aware of this absence of emotion at all times. You may only think about it when you're sitting alone. Or it may be that the feelings are triggered when you're outdoors and hear a particular sound or smell a particular smell. Research has indicated that thinking over and over (ruminating) about what you are (or are not) feeling is not helpful. Learn to focus your attention on the external world. Focus on something outside of yourself and how you feel. Concentrate instead on the task at hand.

There may also be variations in your experiences that you are not aware of at the moment. Again, through careful completion of a diary you will become aware of patterns of thoughts, moods and behaviors and will be able to build up your own psychological model. This model building is important to specify exactly what DPAFU feels like to you.

Thinking in new ways: Challenging your thoughts

One of the key components of CBT is the recognition of unhelpful or negative thoughts. Negative thoughts are often *automatic*; they pop into your head immediately and of their own accord. One negative thought often sets off a chain of others. The thoughts are distorted and/or unhelpful because they help maintain negative moods and may contain one or more cognitive errors as described earlier. They are also involuntary and out of your control so you can't just switch them off or stop them. In fact, trying to stop these thoughts has the opposite effect. It tends to make you think about things longer than if you were to pay little or no attention to them and let them pass through. And negative thoughts appear logical and plausible. For all these reasons we tend to believe in our negative automatic thoughts and may not question their truthfulness. But it is important to remember they are just one possible explanation and there will always be other, alternative ways of looking at things.

This section is specifically designed to help you identify some of the negative thinking that accompanies your DPAFU. As you've worked through the previous sections you may have kept a diary and/or tried to fit your personal experience of DPAFU into the general psychological model described. Many of the negative automatic thoughts you have pop into your head without you giving them very much consideration. Research has shown that having negative thoughts can affect your mood. You won't be surprised to learn that thoughts that focus on potential loss of control, loss of your effectiveness as a person and loss of sensations and emotions, result in a lowered mood. Thoughts of perceived danger, on the other hand, tend to lead to worry and anxiety.

Aaron Beck, the founder of CBT, observed that cognitive distortions or errors are common to all people. However, most of the time people are able to counter or challenge these negative thoughts relatively quickly before becoming distressed by them. But sometimes it can be harder to challenge negative thoughts. This is especially so if you've experienced adverse events, such as trauma or illness, that may have resulted in mental health problems or low self-esteem. We all experience negative thoughts and emotions. Sometimes these are for very good reasons, but if negative automatic thoughts happen too often they can be problematic. They can cause you to have very strong negative emotions that last for a long time.

CBT approaches are based on *measurement*. Think back to when we asked you to attach a numerical value to the sensations or symptoms you experience as part of your DPAFU. In the same way, you can rate or give a numerical value to the strength of your belief that something is true. For example, suppose you were asked how much you believed your eye colour to be blue. Those of you with blue eyes would say 100 per cent true, while those of you with brown or green eyes would say 0 per cent true. That's a fairly straightforward example, but what about things that are not so clear-cut? Imagine you were asked to rate whether a Prime Minister is a good person. This would be difficult to answer with a 0 or 100 per cent. And everyone would be entitled to give their own score – there is no right answer. In much the same way, we can rate how much we believe something to be true, for example using a scoring system where 0 means 'not in the slightest' through to 10 meaning 'absolutely no doubt'.

Next, we can see how having negative automatic thoughts affects our mood. These thoughts can be very fleeting, so much so that it is sometimes quite hard to slow the process down enough to capture our thoughts. Despite this, the effect on our mood is often profound and long-lasting. Look at the example in Table 6.11 overleaf. You'll see that having the negative automatic thought, 'There's no point in going out as I never enjoy it', leads to feelings of sadness and hopelessness.

The next step is to think about the evidence that supports your thought. Our thoughts don't emerge from nowhere. We

TABLE 6.11: EXAMPLE OF JAY'S NEGATIVE AUTOMATIC THOUGHT RECORD		
Negative automatic thought	Mood	Evidence to support your belief
There's no point in going out as I never enjoy it. I believe this is 90 per cent true.	Sadness Hopelessness	When I went out last Tuesday I felt really ill and went home early. (Cognitive error of overgeneralization?)

are likely to have a reason for thinking the way we do. However, we rarely examine the evidence to see how strong or valid it is. Instead, with negative automatic thoughts, we tend to just accept that these are true. In order to stop believing our negative automatic thoughts we need to examine them closely, and not simply accept them. Only when you challenge your thoughts do you gain the power to change them – and by changing your thoughts you can change your moods. When you think of the evidence you are using to confirm your belief, check the list on pages 42–44 and see if you are making one or more of the cognitive errors. The table above includes an example to give you a better idea of how this component of CBT works.

You can see how this evidence is a bit weak. Only one piece of evidence is used to support the negative automatic thought and it seems like an overgeneralization.

Once you're able to identify your negative automatic thoughts and the evidence you're using to support them, you need to look for evidence that *challenges* your view. At first you'll find this extremely difficult. Like most skills, it requires practice. Sometimes, it is easier to imagine the evidence another person might give you. Or you could pretend that your thought is in 'court' and has to provide evidence to justify itself. What might the prosecution say to disprove your belief? It can take some time to get used to thinking up an argument against your own beliefs, thoughts, ideas and images, but once you've mastered it the benefits are huge.

Once you have both sets of evidence – for and against – you can weigh them up, taking into account both sides of the argument. This will help you come up with a balanced or alternative thought that summarizes and takes into account *both* sets of evidence. Rate how much you believe this alternative thought to be true as a percentage. Finally, you need to re-evaluate how much you *now* believe your original negative automatic thought in view of the new evidence (see Table 6.12 overleaf and use the blank table on page 93).

Cognitive behavioral therapy is *not* about trying to replace negative views with positive ones! It is about challenging your old views, ideas and beliefs by generating alternative viewpoints and re-evaluating your beliefs in light of the new evidence or your new views.

A word of warning: it can be very difficult to identify negative automatic thoughts when you first start. In treatment with a therapist people are often given the analogy of learning to read. At first it feels slow and difficult to sound out each of the words. We may also need to use our finger to guide us along. Over time we become faster and more fluent. In the end, we are able to spot words at great distances and no longer need our finger to keep our place. Another useful analogy is learning to drive. At first it feels as if there are so many things to remember: gears, brakes, clutch, mirror, indicators etc. But quite quickly things begin to feel more automatic and/or natural so that you don't have to think so hard about each component. In much the same way this is true for monitoring your own automatic thoughts. Once you learn how to spot them, you can then begin to challenge them. Sometimes it is easier to work backwards. If you find yourself feeling an emotion suddenly, out of the blue or very

TABLE 6.12: CHALLENGING JAY'S NEGATIVE AUTOMATIC THOUGHTS

Negative automatic thought (NAT)	Moods	Evidence for	Evidence against	Balanced thought	Strength of original NAT
There's no point in going out. I never enjoy it. I believe this is 90 per cent true.	Sadness Hopelessness	When I went out last Tuesday, I felt really ill and went home early.	I did go to the cinema last month with Jane and had a good time. Even when I felt ill last month I stayed out and by the end of the night I felt better. I enjoyed 5 out of 10 evenings out. That is more than half of the time.	Although I had a bad time last Tuesday, overall I enjoy myself when I am out. I believe this thought to be 80 per cent true.	Following the new evidence, I now believe my original NAT to be only 20 per cent true.

TABLE 6.13: CHALLENGING AUTOMATIC THOUGHTS					
Negative automatic thought (NAT)	Moods	Evidence for	Evidence against	Balanced thought	Strength of original NAT

intensely, stop and try to remember what you were just thinking about. Or you may find that certain situations trigger thoughts or feelings. Try to identify these situations and capture the thoughts, ideas and images that accompany them.

To start with, just try to recognize or become aware of your thoughts, ideas, beliefs and images. For some people this is easier to do while relaxing, perhaps sitting quietly or going for a walk. Once you become aware of your thoughts, you need to decide which ones are unhelpful and leave you feeling upset or worried. Then look through the list of common cognitive errors on pages 42–44. Which, if any, are you making? Next, using tables like Table 6.13, consider how much you believe the thought and think through the evidence you have to believe it.

Once you have started to identify your negative thoughts, ideas or beliefs, and any cognitive errors, you can then set about changing them. One way of doing this is to challenge them. This process is referred to by psychologists as *cognitive restructuring*, and it encourages you to re-evaluate your own thinking. You can do this by acting like a scientist and gathering evidence to support your belief. Once you've done this, you can then begin to generate alternative views. If you get stuck, come back to it when your mood is better. Or ask other people what they would think if they were in a similar situation. Then consider the advantages and disadvantages for each of the ways of thinking. How do these various thoughts, beliefs, ideas and images affect your mood? Are you making cognitive errors? What might be the best way of looking at things?

Have a look at the following example:

I feel that every time I go out socially my DPAFU gets worse so I don't bother to go out now. My workmates used to ask me out all the time but they hardly bother now. I think it's because they don't really like me.

There are several *negative thought patterns* here. Let's take the first statement: 'every time I go out socially my DPAFU gets worse'. *What evidence do you have?* Well, the last time I went out it happened and I think it did the time before that. *Do you have any evidence of when it didn't happen?* Yes, it didn't get worse when I went out for a meal with a friend, and the time I went to the pub straight after work I felt great. The advantage of thinking this way is that if I am ill I won't make a fool of myself by being around other people, and if they don't really like me then I won't be there anyway. But the disadvantages are that I often feel lonely and being in all the time on my own makes me feel depressed. It also means that I tend to dwell on how I feel and why I have this condition.

I'm making the cognitive error of *overgeneralization*. This means that I tend to hang on to negative information and apply it to all situations. *What might be an alternative or more balanced thought?* A better way to look at this situation might be to think that sometimes I'm aware of DPAFU sensations, but sometimes I'm not. At least by going out I cheer myself up, don't go over and over things in my head and don't get more depressed.

The second negative thought is that 'my workmates don't like me'. *What evidence do you have?* Well, they hardly ever ask me to go out with them anymore. Even though I don't really want to go, it does make me feel sad. *Do you have any evidence of when it didn't happen?* Yes, they did ask me to go out two weeks ago for a leaving do, but I said no because I thought I would feel too unwell. The advantages of thinking this way are that if they don't really like me I won't be there, and that they will probably have a better time without me. But the disadvantages are that I often feel lonely and being in all the time on my own makes me feel depressed. And in the past I have had a few good nights out with them. *What might be an alternative or more balanced thought?* I can see that if every time someone asked me out I said no very soon they might stop asking. Not because they didn't like me – just because they assumed I didn't want to go out. I can't possibly know that they would have a better time without me because I wouldn't be there to see. If I think this way then I don't feel so bad. The cognitive error I'm making is a mixture of *emotional reasoning* and *jumping to conclusions*. I often jump to the conclusion that I will feel worse if I go out, but I do have evidence that is not always the case. In fact it is the least likely outcome. Just because I feel something is true doesn't mean that it is!

The main point to note here is that there can be many different explanations for why and how people behave and that we can interpret that behavior in many ways depending on how we're feeling at the time. The key to challenging negative thinking is to examine all of the possible explanations that we (and other people) might be able to come up with to try and get a more balanced viewpoint.

Completing thought records

CBT can offer you some excellent strategies to help you overcome your negative thinking. One of the best of these is called a *thought record*. Thought records are a systematic way of capturing the situation and your mood and thoughts at any given moment. They allow you to look at the evidence for your thoughts and then generate alternative, balanced viewpoints. Filling in a thought record is a bit like putting your negative thoughts on trial. You look at the evidence for, and against, these negative thoughts (rather like the evidence that the prosecution and defence lawyers might produce in a courtroom). Believing totally in your negative thoughts, without looking to see if there are any counter-arguments, is like only having a prosecution lawyer in a trial. Just imagine being in court without a defence lawyer – the jury would only hear one side of the story (the accusations against you) and would find you guilty. That's what it's like if you listen to your negative thoughts without trying to defend yourself. Using a thought record helps you to examine the evidence from which you derive your negative thoughts. It also helps you learn how to challenge this evidence with your own counter-evidence. Only once you have listed both the negative and the positive evidence are you in a position to act as your own judge and jury. This will allow you to come up with a *balanced viewpoint* that takes into account *all* the evidence. (See page 100 for an example.)

In summary, filling in a thought record should include the following steps:

1 In column 1, note down the situation when the thought occurred, including when (i.e. day, date or time), where you were, what you were doing (briefly), and who you were with. Try to picture yourself back in the situation as vividly as possible.

2 In column 2, write down all the emotions that you felt at the time. These should be single words such as sad, angry, hopeless, frightened etc. Try to be as specific as possible. For instance, if you felt distressed, try to unpick what individual moods you were experiencing. Rate each mood state from 0 (not at all) to 100 (the worst you have ever felt or the strongest the emotion could ever be for you). So a score of 50 would mean that you felt the emotion to a moderate or average extent.

3 In column 3, identify the actual negative automatic thought (or NAT) as it came to you. Write this out in as

much detail as possible, as though you were actually speaking or thinking it. If you had an image, try to put down as much as you are able in words. Don't worry if you find it hard to identify the thought immediately. Just let your mind go back to the situation and gradually the thought will come back to you. This thought is likely to be closely linked to the negative emotions you've listed. Record next to the negative automatic thought how strongly you believed it. Rate it as a percentage, i.e. on a scale of 0–100, where 0 means you didn't believe it at all and 100 means that you believed it completely.

4 In column 4, start to question the validity of the negative thought. Write down the evidence you're relying on for thinking this way. Why do you believe this thought? Are you making a cognitive error? Try to record as much evidence as you can. Think about the type of evidence that you would need to produce in a court case and avoid making assumptions or mind-reading, which you would be unable to substantiate.

5 In column 5, start to generate as much counter-evidence against the negative automatic thought as you possibly can. Take your time on this step; the more counter-evidence you can find against your negative automatic thought, the better you'll feel. Look back at the list of cognitive errors. Are you making any of them? Try to identify which ones might apply to your negative automatic thought. Ask yourself the following questions. What could you argue in your defence? Are there any pieces of counter-evidence that you've overlooked? Has the opposite ever happened? How might you think about this when you're feeling better? What would you say to someone else who was thinking this? Try to come up with as many alternative viewpoints as you possibly can. Once you've generated as many alternatives as you

can on your own, you may wish to ask other people for their opinions.

6 Once you have listed all the evidence for, and against, your negative automatic thought, read through the lists in columns 4 and 5. Next, think of your *balanced or alternative thought*. Using the metaphor of a legal trial, this is similar to the judge summing up the evidence for the jury to make their decision. Write this in Column 6 and rate how strongly you believe this statement as an alternative explanation. Again do this on a scale of 0–100, with 0 meaning you do not believe it at all and 100 meaning you believe it totally.

7 Re-rate the strength of the old negative automatic thought in light of new evidence and alternative explanations. Try to be honest here, and remember all the cognitive errors and biases that can occur. Your rating will usually decrease. The reduction is often small at first but it will become greater as you become more used to challenging your own thoughts and their meanings. This takes hard work and practice. Finally, holding your new balanced thought in your mind, go back to the list of negative emotions you experienced during the situation. Do these feel less intense? Would your rate them lower now that you have looked at all the counter-evidence?

As before, you'll find a completed record on page 100 as an example to help you. There are also blank copies so that you can complete your own, one on page 101 and one in Appendix III.

Be patient with yourself

Please bear in mind that it can be very difficult to come up with alternative and more helpful thoughts when you're

TABLE 6.14: EXAMPLE THOUGHT RECORD

1. Situation (when/where/what/with whom)	2. Moods strength (0–100%)	3. Negative automatic thought (NAT) and strength of belief (0–100%)	4. Evidence for the NAT	5. Evidence against the NAT	6. Alternative or balanced thought and strength of belief (0–100%)	7. Strength of old NAT (0–100%)
Mon 11 Nov 8 p.m. In my living room. Sitting watching TV, on my own.	Sad 80% Angry 50%	What was the point of trying to get help. I have read the book and my DPAFU is exactly the same. 100%	I still feel the same. I just noticed I am still seeing floaters. I don't feel more 'real'. I don't feel any more connected to my wife.	I have only just started using the book and I have only skim-read a couple of bits. I should go back and take my time. I have only tried out a couple of exercises. The idea of self-help is about self-management and the changes I can make more time for myself. At least I am watching TV; this time last year I didn't even watch it. It is unrealistic to expect a cure so soon. That was really my goal but it is not achievable in such a short space of time. It may happen in the future but I should not set up false or unachievable goals. I need to think about other ways of monitoring change that aren't based on how I feel emotionally.	I still have some DPAFU but I have started to try to help myself and need to give myself more time for things to change. 80%	50%

TABLE 6.15: THOUGHT RECORD

1. Situation (when/ where/what/ with whom)	2. Moods strength (0–100%)	3. Negative automatic thought (NAT) and strength of belief (0–100%)	4. Evidence for the NAT	5. Evidence against the NAT	6. Alternative or balanced thought and strength of belief (0–100%)	7. Strength of old NAT (0–100%)

feeling low or anxious. You may want to write the thoughts down and come back to them at a later date. You may also want to ask others – perhaps a friend or work colleague – what they would think in the same situation. Or you could carry out a survey to get a wider viewpoint: ask lots of people for their ideas about the situation you encountered to see how they would interpret it. Be alert to the possibility that you're being self-critical or dismissing other points of view because you believe people are only saying things to make you feel better or to keep you happy. This is a cognitive error known as *discounting the positive*.

Like so much else in CBT, you don't have to be perfect at thought records. There are no right and wrong answers. It is about you challenging your own thoughts. Don't give up, even if you find the task hard or if you find that you're having the same thoughts time after time. This is completely normal; negative thoughts tend to reappear again and again. After all, that's what keeps the negative cycle going.

Thought records are extremely important and they're central to your self-management of DPAFU. By recognizing your unhelpful thoughts and the impact they have on your mood and behavior, you can begin to challenge and generate alternative ways of looking at things. This includes your beliefs, the meaning of your symptoms and experiences, and how you respond to these. Like much of this book, it's a subject that you may want to go back and read about several times. You'll also need to practise keeping thought records. We all sometimes find ourselves dismissing something as useless because it didn't work immediately. You might want to use the example on page 100 as a template.

Behaving in new ways: Tackling your avoidance and safety-seeking behaviors

Earlier we saw how DPAFU sensations can make you behave in particular ways, for instance by avoiding situations or by adopting strategies that you feel help you cope (*safety-seeking behaviors*). We also considered how these might actually help continue your problems or even make them worse. In order to break this negative cycle you will need to actively tackle these behaviors. The way to do this is to first *create a hierarchy* of such behaviors. Then these can be challenged with the use of *behavioral experiments*.

How to create a hierarchy of the behaviors you want to change

Some of the earlier exercises will have helped you identify already the negative behaviors (avoidances and safety-seeking behaviors) that are associated with your DPAFU. For example, look in the sections entitled 'Assessing the impact DPAFU has on your life' (page 59), 'Diary keeping' (page 71) and 'Building an explanation that fits' (page 84). Write a list of all of the behaviors you noted in these sections on the lines below:

Avoidances

Safety-seeking behaviors

Next, look through your list and rate each behavior in terms of: (1) how difficult you would find it to do (if it is something you avoid); or (2) how difficult you would find it to *not* do (if it is a safety-seeking behavior that gives you a sense of comfort). Use the scale of 0–10 given below and write a number next to each behavior on the list you have created.

0 . . . 1 . . . 2 . . . 3 . . . 4 . . . 5 . . . 6 . . . 7 . . . 8 . . . 9 . . . 10

Not difficult at all	Moderately difficult	Very difficult indeed

Now write out the list again, on the lines below. But this time re-order the behaviors by placing the behavior with the highest number at the top, and working down through the list so that the lowest number is at the bottom. This is your personal hierarchy of avoidance and/or safety-seeking behaviors.

Avoidance   Difficulty rating to do this

Safety-seeking behavior   Difficulty rating to *not* do this

Example: Mina's hierarchy

Avoidance	Difficulty rating to do this
Driving	10
Spending time around people	8
Looking at reflections of myself	6
Safety-seeking behavior	**Difficulty rating to *not* do this**
Pinch myself to see if I can feel	7
Only go supermarket shopping very early in the morning when it is quiet	5
Check my eyesight for visual disturbances	4

Finding out about your underlying assumptions

Behavioral experiments are ways of testing out the thoughts, beliefs and assumptions that underlie your avoidances and safety-seeking behaviors. In order to change the behavior, you first need to identify the assumptions that cause it. Then you can challenge these assumptions, much in the same way as you did when you used a thought record. However, with thought records you challenged the negative automatic thought just by *thinking* of counter-evidence. However, in a behavioral experiment you need to *actively do something* to challenge your thoughts. First, you set up your assumptions in the form of a prediction. Next you devise an experiment to test whether what you believe (i.e. your negative assumptions) does or doesn't come true in real life.

Let's use the example of Mina. In her hierarchy of avoidances and safety-seeking behaviors, Mina rated driving as 10/10 in terms of difficulty. In other words, she saw driving as the most difficult thing she could do given her DPAFU.

But we need to understand *why* driving is so difficult for her. Not everyone will have the same underlying reasons to explain their behavior, even if the behavior is the same. One person may avoid driving because they feel they won't be able to see properly. Someone else may avoid driving because they think they will become too anxious. Another person may avoid it because they are convinced they will have an accident. The behavior (i.e. avoiding driving) is the same, but the beliefs underlying it differ.

In order to find out what beliefs are causing you to behave in certain ways, choose one of the behaviors you want to change and ask yourself the following questions:

* What do you think might happen if you didn't behave in this way? (*For safety-seeking behaviors*)
* What would be the *worst* thing that could happen if you didn't behave in this way? (*For safety-seeking behaviors*)
* What do you think might happen if you behaved in this way? (*For avoidance*)
* What do you think would be the *worst* thing that could happen if you behaved in this way? (*For avoidance*)
* What images come to mind when you picture behaving, or not behaving, in this way?
* What would the worst outcome mean to you?
* What would the worst outcome say about you as a person?
* What would be so bad about that?

Keep repeating the above questions in any order until you reach what you feel is at the root cause of your behavior. This is called the *downward arrow* technique.

So for Mina's example of avoiding driving, the exercise might go as follows:

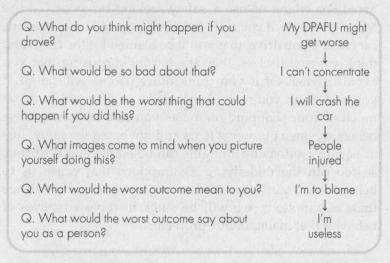

Q. What do you think might happen if you drove?	My DPAFU might get worse
Q. What would be so bad about that?	I can't concentrate
Q. What would be the *worst* thing that could happen if you did this?	I will crash the car
Q. What images come to mind when you picture yourself doing this?	People injured
Q. What would the worst outcome mean to you?	I'm to blame
Q. What would the worst outcome say about you as a person?	I'm useless

Here's another example, this time using the downward arrow technique with Mina's safety-seeking behavior of only going to the supermarket very early in the morning when it's quiet:

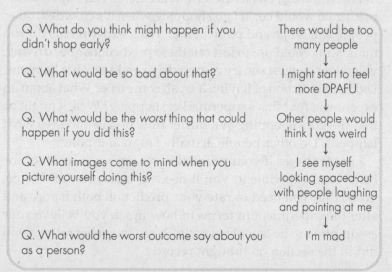

Q. What do you think might happen if you didn't shop early?	There would be too many people
Q. What would be so bad about that?	I might start to feel more DPAFU
Q. What would be the *worst* thing that could happen if you did this?	Other people would think I was weird
Q. What images come to mind when you picture yourself doing this?	I see myself looking spaced-out with people laughing and pointing at me
Q. What would the worst outcome say about you as a person?	I'm mad

Once you have identified the core belief underlying your behavior, it will become very clear as to why you want to avoid something or use a safety-seeking behavior. To use Mina's example, if you truly believe that you'll have a serious car crash if you drive, that you'll be blamed for the crash and think yourself useless, then it's hardly surprising that you avoid driving. Or if you think other people will laugh at you and think you're mad, naturally you'll want to do as much of your shopping online as you can. However, these beliefs are often our worst fears and not based in reality. Just as negative automatic thoughts can be biased and distorted, so too can the underlying assumptions that cause us to behave in certain ways. Unless we test out and challenge these assumptions, we will be stuck in repeated cycles of behavior that maintain our problems.

Devising behavioral experiments

Using the examples above, Mina's driving prediction would be: 'If I drive the car, I'll have a serious accident.' Her supermarket prediction would be: 'If I go shopping when it's crowded, other people will laugh and point at me.' What experiments do you think Mina could use to test out these predictions? For driving, you might suggest she try a short drive and see what happens. Did her prediction of having a crash come true? What about an experiment for Mina's supermarket shopping? Well, it might be that she goes shopping at a busier time of day and sees what happens. Do other people actually laugh and point?

In order to see if your prediction changes as a result of the behavioral experiment, you'll need to measure the change. To do this, you need to rate your prediction both before and after the experiment in terms of how much you believe your assumption to be true. This is similar to the belief ratings you did in the section on thought records.

```
0 .. 10 .. 20 .. 30 .. 40 .. 50 .. 60 .. 70 .. 80 .. 90 .. 100

Don't                    Moderately                    Totally
believe                  convinced                     convinced
it at all
```

You might already be able to see a difficulty in setting up behavioral experiments. If you believe something terrible will happen if you do something, or alternatively if you don't do something, you're probably going to be very worried about testing it out. So it's important to make the behavioral experiment easy enough for you to go ahead and try it out. In the case of driving, you might suggest Mina start with a very short drive on a quiet bit of road. For the supermarket, you might want her to go at a time when it's likely to be only a little bit busier. Start with relatively easy experiments. Just by doing them you'll build up your confidence. Don't try to do too much at once. Some simple ways you can make things easier for yourself might include:

- Starting with something that is rated low on your hierarchy – you'll find this easier to challenge.
- Trying things for very short periods to begin with, and then gradually increasing the time.
- Testing things out with people who don't know you or, alternatively, who know you well and understand your problems.
- Trying your experiment with the help of a friend, partner or family member before doing it on your own.
- Thinking carefully beforehand about how you can make the experiment a bit easier for yourself.

Here's what you need to do to set up a successful behavioral experiment:

1 Identify your target avoidance or safety-seeking behaviors.
2 Rate each of these in terms of how difficult it would be to do or to stop doing.
3 Build a hierarchy with the most difficult at the top and the easiest at the bottom.
4 Choose something easy to start with.
5 Identify your underlying assumption using the downward arrow technique.
6 Try to be as precise as possible about your belief.
7 Rate how much you believe in your prediction.
8 Devise a behavioral experiment that will test out your prediction.
9 Carry out the experiment!
10 Compare the actual result to the result you predicted. How accurate was your prediction?
11 Re-rate your belief if your prediction did not come true. Modify if necessary.
12 Ask yourself what you have learnt from this experiment.

On page 111 is an example worksheet for a behavioral experiment and on page 112 a blank one that you can complete for your own experiments. You'll find another blank copy in Appendix III.

You'll see from these examples that Mina's belief in her original assumption was a bit lower after she carried out the behavioral experiments than before. Don't worry if your belief rating doesn't reduce a great deal. To achieve this, you're likely to need to set up several experiments that gradually increase in difficulty. Often, even if an experiment

TABLE 6.16: EXAMPLE BEHAVIORAL EXPERIMENT WORKSHEET: MINA

Target behavior	Assumption being tested	Belief in assumption (%)	Experiment	Outcome of experiment	New belief in assumption (%)
Avoiding driving.	If I drive the car, then I will have a serious accident.	90%	Drive for 20 minutes along quiet roads with my sister in the car.	Nothing happened. My sister told me she thought I was a good driver.	70%
Shopping early in the morning when it is quiet.	If I go shopping when it is crowded, then other people will laugh and point at me.	75%	Go into supermarket at lunchtime and buy a sandwich.	Some teenagers were laughing but I don't think it was at me. Most people were too busy to notice me.	80%

TABLE 6.17: BEHAVIORAL EXPERIMENT WORKSHEET

Target behavior	Assumption being tested	Belief in assumption (%)	Experiment	Outcome of experiment	New belief in assumption (%)

has been successful, you may find that you think of a 'yes, but' type statement that provides an excuse for why it worked out this time. For instance, in the example above, Mina felt that an accident was only prevented because her sister was there and kept talking to her as she drove. She also thought that people didn't laugh at her in the supermarket because it was lunchtime and they were all in a hurry. Can you think of further experiments that she could try in order to test these beliefs out? Perhaps she would need to drive again without her sister talking to her. Perhaps she could try driving on her own. Perhaps she needs to go to the supermarket in the evening when it might be busy but people wouldn't be in a hurry. Look out for any 'yes, but' thoughts you have that seem to diminish the effectiveness of your own experiment. Set up another experiment to test your new prediction.

Reducing symptom monitoring

One of the most common traps that people with DPAFU fall into is constantly monitoring their DPAFU to see if it is getting worse. This is understandable. But if you look back at Figure 4.5 on page 35, you'll see that regular scanning and monitoring of symptoms is likely to result in several unwanted consequences:

- A negative impact on your mood (such as increasing worry and apprehensiveness).
- A worsening of the negative interpretations you might have for the meaning of your sensations.
- A greater sense of feeling disconnected from the outside world.

In other words, the more attention you give to your DPAFU, and the more you focus on what is happening inside your body, the more you will increase and maintain your DPAFU.

Research studies support this idea. People who have hypochondriasis, or anxiety about their health, may worry that they may have some serious disease (such as cancer). They then spend lots of time scanning their body for any sensations that they believe could be the first signs of danger. Similarly, people who experience panic attacks commonly monitor their body so that they are prepared if they start to feel panic. Unfortunately, this increased physical monitoring means that you are more likely to notice sensations that are completely harmless. If instead your attention was focused on what you were doing, or on your external environment, you wouldn't actually notice these symptoms. The more we notice these harmless sensations, we more go on to notice them in the future – and the more severe we think they are. This then creates another of those vicious cycles. And though this example is for hypochondriasis, the same applies to monitoring symptoms of DPAFU.

On the other hand, research has found that if someone concentrates hard on something in the external environment, such as trying to solve a difficult puzzle, their attention to their symptoms is massively reduced. They then report their sensations as significantly less problematic. As a result, people often say that their DPAFU is at its best when they get involved in something that takes their mind off how they are feeling.

TRY THIS EXPERIMENT

Pick one of the sensations of DPAFU that you are currently experiencing, or focus on any part of your body (e.g. one of your hands or feet). Shut your eyes for a few minutes and concentrate totally on your sensations. See what you notice. Did the sensations change when you were concentrating on them? Did you notice any new sensations? Did the original sensations increase in intensity?

Now try some mental arithmetic. Starting from the number 200, try subtracting the number 7 repeatedly from the number you obtain, e.g. 193, 186, 179, and so forth until you reach 0. When you stop counting, reflect on your sensations of DPAFU while you were doing the mental arithmetic. Did you notice the sensations as much when you were doing the arithmetic? Or did you find that your mind was so absorbed in concentration that the sensations felt less intense?

One technique that people with DPAFU find useful is an exercise that helps you shift your attention. Rather than focusing inwards on how you are feeling physically, mentally and emotionally, the idea is instead to shift the focus to the outside world. This means paying attention to what is happening around you. It's a particularly useful technique because we know that people with DPAFU spend a lot of time reflecting on how they are feeling. This can include spending time thinking about thoughts and sensations and/or focusing on how to overcome DPAFU. It's not surprising that if you spend lots of time thinking about yourself, you're paying less attention to the external world. This will magnify the sensation of being detached and cut off.

Imagine that each of us has 100 units in our mind to process everything that occurs. We may use 10 units of these to process peripheral sound and vision. Another 10 units might be used to focus on how we feel. If we find we are hungry or thirsty, we may use 10 units to think about what we are going to cook for dinner that night. This leaves 70 units to focus on the task at hand. Now imagine that out of 100 units we are using 30 or 40 to focus on how we are feeling inside, including how spaced out or detached we feel. We've reduced the number of available processing units down to 30 or 40. Bearing this in mind, it's inevitable that people with DPAFU will frequently report difficulty with attention and concentration.

A psychologist called Adrian Wells developed a specific technique called *attention training* to help change the focus of our attention. The technique was originally intended to be delivered by a therapist, but the exercise we're presenting here is a shortened version for you to practise on your own. As you sit in a room, try to become aware of three distinct sounds. The first should be something that is immediate and close by within the room. You may have to introduce something such as a ticking clock. The second sound should be something that is just outside the room, perhaps something from another room or outside your house or office. The third sound should be something that is in the far distance, such as the noise of traffic outside. Make sure you have three distinct sounds and try to focus on each one in turn. Practise becoming aware of each sound. Once you are practised at recognizing these different sounds, start to switch your attention between the three.

It may help if you pre-record a cassette giving yourself these instructions, in the same way as a therapist would guide you through the exercise. For instance, ask yourself to switch from sounds in the room to the sounds outside, and then to the sounds in the distance. Then back again to sounds outside, to sounds in the room etc. You don't have to follow any particular sequence. As you become more familiar with the exercise, try to notice as many sounds as you can at once. You'll find that one sound usually takes precedence over the others. It may be very difficult to divide your attention and listen to the sounds simultaneously.

Practise this exercise for five to 10 minutes, twice a day. Continue until you're able to switch your attention rapidly from internal thoughts and feelings to the external sounds and stimuli. Although this technique is not intended to be used in times of distress, it can also work as a distraction technique at these times. At first, however, you should try to do this exercise when you're feeling calm and relatively relaxed. As with the other new skills you're learning, it will take time and practice. As you progress, you may prefer to switch your attention not just to sounds, but to smells or visual cues such as colours. In fact, you can use any stimuli that are outside of your internal world and in the external environment instead. Many sufferers have reported that this technique can help them feel less isolated, detached or cut off from the 'real' world. This is because their attention is now actively focused on the external environment.

Managing your own treatment

This book is all about helping you to better manage aspects of your DPAFU. In order to do that you will need to reflect on what you believe about DPAFU. Think about the factors that caused it and those that lead to it continuing. How does it cause problems in your life, or do the problems in your life cause DPAFU? This is a good point at which to review the model in Figure 4.5 (see page 35) and think about how each of the components fits with your experience. It may be that you believe that DPAFU has caused some sort of irreversible brain damage (although our research does not bear this out). This may mean you may believe that the possibility of psychological treatment working will be slim. You may be looking for a 'chemical cure' or indeed may actually believe that there is nothing that can be done.

Having to choose between *either* a biological or a psychological explanation is not necessary. The two are not mutually exclusive and in fact they complement each other. Remember that thoughts can influence the brain, just as the brain can influence thoughts. In fact for some people the best treatment appears to be a combination of the psychological and biological approaches. There have been very good success rates for people who have taken medication and had cognitive behavioral therapy at the same time. By 'success rates', we don't just mean a decrease in, or a cure of, DPAFU sensations. Success can come in all shapes and forms. For some, it's about returning to work or being able to do the things they used to enjoy, while for others it's about improving the quality of their relationships.

Like any form of intervention, self-help books can lead to some people feeling as if things are getting worse. This may be because you are beginning to address thoughts, ideas or beliefs that have been difficult to deal with or that you may not have been aware of before now. Also, the very act of thinking about DPAFU can *initially* make it feel much more intense for some people. A number of research studies have confirmed this to be the case.

At this point it may be worth going back over the previous sections trying to be more specific in your definition and assessment of your problems. This will make SMART (specific, measurable, achievable, realistic and time limited) goal-setting easier. Once your problems are defined and your goals set, you can go to each of the relevant sections to look for helpful tips. For instance, if you've identified your main problem as negative thought patterns leading to low mood, anxiety and low self-confidence, you'll find lots of useful material in the sections on thinking in new ways; managing anxiety, worry and DPAFU; low mood and DPAFU; and low self-esteem. Don't feel that you have to work through the sections in the order they appear in the book. The idea of self-help is that you can access areas of help as and when you need it, and we want you to dip in and out of this book as and when needed. It may be helpful for you to make notes or jot down your thoughts as you read through each section. You can go back over these notes later to monitor change, and/or clarify issues or ideas that you didn't understand or points that you strongly relate to.

Bear in mind that each of the following sections focuses specifically on DPAFU. We'll sometimes recommend more general self-help books, but we don't supply an exhaustive list. And remember that not every section will be relevant to you or how you are feeling.

Worry, anxiety and DPAFU

We're now going to look at the anxiety and worry associated with DPAFU. These worries can be specific, for example worrying about what caused the DPAFU in the first place or what the end result might be. Or the worries may be more general, for example worrying about your future or the state of the world. Of course, you might also worry about your thoughts and worries. Whatever your concerns, we hope the following pages will help.

This section is only a brief, DPAFU-focused overview of the vast amount of literature on worry and anxiety currently available. If you feel that your anxiety is not specifically related to DPAFU, you may benefit from a self-help guide aimed specifically at managing panic and anxiety. We recommend some of these in the section on further reading at the end of the book. Also have a look at Chapter 7 for other techniques that can be helpful. These include problem-solving skills to help you deal more effectively with decision-making and relaxation and mindfulness techniques.

One of the key ways of managing anxiety is to become aware of what exactly it is that you are worried about. What are the thoughts that go round and round in your head? Are they about the same subject? Psychologists call these repetitive, intrusive and unwanted thoughts *ruminations*. People often find themselves going over and over the same worries because they believe that eventually they'll be able to work them through. But going over and over the same thoughts often leaves you feeling as if you're going to drive yourself mad. Worrying can actually be very unhelpful. Often people worry about things that have happened in the past or dwell on what might have happened if things had been done differently. But of course the past can't be changed by worrying about it.

People also worry about how to prevent bad things happening in the future. Sometimes it's helpful to separate out your worries about the past from your anxieties about the future; it's part of trying to be clear about what's behind your feelings of anxiety or uneasiness. Events that have happened in the past can't be changed, as we've said, and going over and over them in your mind often leads to further feelings of anxiety and low mood. Clearly this is not a helpful strategy. Likewise when we go over all of the things that could possibly happen to us in the future, we often feel increased anxiety and stress. Again the aim here is to adopt a more balanced viewpoint. Ask yourself how likely it is that something bad will happen, and be careful that you are not using *emotional reasoning* (one of the cognitive errors) to justify how you feel. Imagine that you believed very strongly that the most likely thing to happen when you left the house that day was that you would be abducted by aliens! It's not likely that many of us would choose to leave the house – no matter how unlikely it was – if we believed this to be 100 per cent true, but how might we behave if we believed it to be 40 per cent true? Well, we might leave the house but remain vigilant. What if we believed it was 1 per cent likely? Then we would probably not give it a second thought. It's important to spend some time identifying the types of worries and anxieties you have as they very often have a significant impact on our behavior.

Some of the techniques used by people suffering from general worry and anxiety can help here. First you need to allocate some *dedicated worry time.* Half an hour per day is usually plenty. Plan this dedicated worry time for a time of day that suits you best, for example when you return from work, after you've eaten dinner or when the children are in bed. Stick to the same time every day. When you find yourself starting to worry, say to yourself that you will deal with this later during your worry time and that thinking about it now will not help. Like all of the other suggestions and exercises in this book, this one will take time and practice to master.

For your first worry session you'll need a sheet of paper and a pen. A postcard will be enough once you're used to the technique. Make a note of the worry or anxiety that bothers you the most. Then begin to challenge the worry in much the same way as you did with the thought records. Imagine what other people might say. Look at what evidence you have. Are there any alternative ideas, thoughts and beliefs? What can you begin to do to address each worry? Write your responses underneath the worry. Try to fit each worry onto one sheet or card. At the end of the half hour, just stop. You can come back to the worry again the next day. Try to identify and tackle a different worry during each worry time. You'll be surprised at how similar many of the worries are.

EXAMPLE WORRY CARD

My DPAFU can't be cured and I'll be like this forever

I don't know that for a fact. It just feels that way. I'm using emotional reasoning and that is prone to error.

Even if it doesn't go away completely I can manage it better. Then the impact it has on my life will be minimal.

I've read on a website that it does go away for some people when they stop worrying about it.

Going over and over it in my head is not going to help; if anything it'll make things worse.

I am going to practise attention training as a way of trying to stop me focusing on my symptoms.

Eventually you'll have a set of worry cards that cover all of the issues that cause you worry or anxiety. This means that when you have a specific or general worry you'll be able to turn to the card and look at what you've written. You may wish to add more each time or remove the things that are no longer applicable. Over time you'll become more practised in your responses to your worries and will begin to know them off by heart. Then when the worry pops into your head you'll have an automatic response. Gradually, your worries will become fewer as you postpone them until worry time. This will mean you'll be able to deal with them quickly and effectively. Like many of the exercises in this book, you can ask other people – maybe friends, family or work colleagues – how they might respond to a given worry or anxiety. You can then incorporate their answers into your own to help you generate new ways of thinking. You can also rewrite the cards as your ideas and thoughts change. For example, after reading the section on problem-solving you may wish to draw up a list of the advantages (benefits) and disadvantages (costs) of having such a worry, or what it means to you if you don't worry.

It may be that your worries are not ruminatory, but instead come out of the blue. These may make you feel much more anxious – even to the extent of provoking what seems like a panic attack. It can be very difficult to tease apart DPAFU from panic. Research has shown that more than half of people who suffer with panic attacks become depersonalized during the attack. In turn, about half of the people who suffer with DPAFU also have panic attacks.

If you suffer from panic attacks on a regular basis, you might want to get some help that's specifically targeted at that problem. You could use self-help books. Or you might visit your GP and ask for a referral for CBT for panic from your local psychology and counselling service. This treatment is very effective and well-established. If you only suffer with panic rarely, or find yourself getting anxious or worried before a specific event or situation, such as a night out with friends, then this section may be of benefit to you. Many of the symptoms or sensations associated with panic are the same as DPAFU. For example, the usual sensations of panic are:

- increased heart rate
- increased breathing
- dry mouth
- feeling dizzy, faint, hot, or sweaty
- feeling cut off, detached, or light-headed
- distorted vision
- mind racing
- confusion
- thoughts of losing control and going mad
- feeling frightened

Usually with panic, a trigger sets off a chain reaction. The trigger can be a physical sensation, a distressing thought or even the dread of another panic attack. This then leads to the person feeling afraid or anxious or worried. When you feel like this, and you have all of the bodily sensations detailed above, this can lead to thoughts of disaster or a sense that something terrible or sinister is going to happen. These feelings are then taken as further proof that it will definitely happen. Such thoughts usually centre around the fear of losing control, going mad and/or dying.

Increased heart rate	→	I'm having a heart attack
Breathlessness	→	I'm going to suffocate
Feeling unreal	→	I'm going mad
Feeling distant or cut off	→	I've got brain damage or schizophrenia

Once this chain reaction begins and thoughts become 'catastrophic', the anxiety continues. This is because of the adrenaline that the body produces. You may feel petrified and your body continues to react as it should under conditions of terror i.e. increased heart rate and the usual sensations of anxiety. Once again a vicious cycle is in action.

Just as you did for the psychological model we outlined in Chapter 4, you'll need to think how your experiences fit this model of the process of anxiety, worry and panic. This will give you a clearer picture of what happens to you during a panic attack. Once you can predict what sensation, thought or image follows on from another, you'll probably feel less frightened. This is because your understanding will grow. You'll need to identify when the panic occurred and what was happening at the time. For example, is there a trigger that is specific to certain places? What were you thinking at the time? It may not be until afterwards that you realize you were thinking about something in particular. Did you become aware of a certain physical sensation, such as a missed heartbeat? (Many people don't know that our heart doesn't beat regularly all day. It often speeds up or slows down for no apparent reason. But this can feel really scary.) What were you doing? Record these things as soon as possible after each attack while it's still fresh in your mind. Concentrate on the worst sensation. What did you think was going to happen? If you thought you were going to die, go mad or collapse, why didn't it actually happen? What did you do to stop it? Were there things you did or said in your mind to stop the worst case scenario from happening?

It's likely that over time you have collected evidence to support the worst case scenario i.e. that you are about to lose control, go mad or develop schizophrenia etc. You may feel that you've had a narrow escape. But how do you account for the fact that the worst hasn't happened so far? Think about this as evidence in itself. What alternative explanations might there be for your sensations? Are there people or places you avoid because you believe that they make things worse? How realistic is that belief? It could be that it's true, or it could simply be that you *think* it's true. As we've already seen, there's a difference! Try to be aware too of the mental images or pictures you have when you feel panicky. These images may be particularly awful and upsetting. If you push them away and don't deal with them at the time, they may make the problem continue. You'd be left with a feeling of something awful, although you may not be sure of what exactly it is.

Panic is no different to DPAFU; the more you worry about it, the more likely you are to notice the sensations that support it. What are the sensations that really bother you? What do they mean? Do you have evidence to support your beliefs? What might a logical argument against your beliefs be like? You may wish to include in your logical arguments some of these facts about panic:

- During a panic attack, it's virtually impossible to faint because your heart is beating fast and your blood pressure is increased.
- Panic is caused by fear and kept going by adrenaline.
- Adrenaline makes your heart beat faster and your lungs breathe harder. It diverts the blood supply to where you may need it for urgent action (e.g. the muscles) and away from where it's not quite so necessary (e.g. the gut – leading to 'butterflies in the stomach'). In evolutionary terms, this is called the 'fight or flight response'. You feel dizzy and faint because you're breathing too hard and exhaling carbon dioxide. This makes the blood vessels to your brain contract, which makes you light-headed.
- The more you worry, the more sensations you notice.
- The more sensations you notice, the more you will worry.
- Noticing sensations confirms your belief that something is wrong. This is the cognitive error of emotional reasoning. Just because you believe or feel something to be true doesn't mean that it is.
- If the worst thing that could happen has not happened by now, that's because it is not going to.
- If you do something to stop the panic getting out of hand, such as having a sip of water or sitting down, you'll believe it's the sip of water or the act of sitting down that stopped you from suffocating or collapsing. Again, these are safety behaviors and they may stop you seeing that the worst simply would not have happened even if you hadn't intervened.

Just as you did with the thought records, write down your thoughts, ideas, beliefs and images and challenge the evidence you have to support them. Then start generating alternative or more balanced viewpoints. Once again, rate how strongly you believe the thought using the same scale you used before.

We should also mention *anticipatory* anxiety, when you become anxious before anything has happened, and *social* anxiety, when you worry about social situations in which you feel that you may be judged. It may well be that you suffer from these forms of anxiety in addition to DPAFU. If you recognize these feelings, we suggest you ask your GP for help or investigate self-help. Once again, CBT has a good track record in successfully treating these conditions. There are also some useful self-help books available to help you manage social anxiety.

Low mood and DPAFU

In this section we look at low mood associated with DPAFU, and not low mood in its own right. If you think you may be suffering from depression, our advice would be to consult your GP and/or a good self-help guide, for example *Overcoming Depression* by Paul Gilbert (2000) or *Mind Over Mood* by Dennis Greenberger and Christine Padesky (1995). There are numerous others and a quick visit to the self-help section of a bookshop or an Internet search will give you lots of other possibilities.

Like any other chronic condition, DPAFU can get you down and often leads to feelings of hopelessness about the future (we saw this with Alexi's case history, see page 19). You may wonder whether you'll ever feel well again, which of course is likely to lower your mood. Some people also feel helpless because they believe there's very little that can be done to make things better. Low mood doesn't just mean you feel sad; it can affect you on a variety of levels. It can leave you with disturbed sleep, a feeling of exhaustion, irritableness, poor appetite and constant worry. It can make you avoid other people and make you much more prone to cognitive errors (see page 42). People think many of these sensations or symptoms are caused by DPAFU. But low mood and DPAFU aren't one and the same, although there is little doubt that they are related.

Research has shown that we're all sometimes liable to *negative automatic thoughts* and the *cognitive errors* they generally involve. Most of the time, the impact cognitive errors have on our mood, physical reactions and behaviors is minimal. By and large, they do little damage and go unnoticed. But they may become more frequent, prominent, and distressing – perhaps following a critical incident, the onset of another condition or as a reaction to an event in our lives. In the negative cycle that follows, the depressed person believes that nothing they do will make them feel better so they no longer bother to try. There is a general feeling of despondency. Hence the old expression that the glass is half empty.

It is these very negative thought-behavior-mood cycles that people with DPAFU often find themselves caught up in. The way to address low mood is initially to recognize it. Is your mood a cause of DPAFU or a consequence? Are you depressed irrespective of the DPAFU? The first question is very difficult to answer. For some people, low mood will have followed the onset of the DPAFU. You will then need to become aware of the thoughts you have about DPAFU. We know that depression often occurs as a result of perceived loss. Are you grieving for the loss of your old self? Do you feel that you have no control over the sensations of DPAFU and that the situation is hopeless? Do you believe that the DPAFU is a result of, or has caused, irreversible brain damage and that there is nothing you can do about it? All these thoughts and feelings may exaggerate feelings of help-lessness. Either way, these are negative thoughts that you can list in a thought record (see page 101). Remember to gather evidence to support or refute your beliefs.

By drawing on CBT models, you can guide your treatment and devise your own self-help program. You can work to change any one of the five systems outlined earlier in Figure 5.1 (see page 47). For instance, you can change:

- how you *think* (through the use of thought records);
- how you *feel physically* (you can tackle issues like sleep, diet and exercise or use antidepressant medication);
- change your *environment* (for example, by going away on holiday);
- how you *feel emotionally* (this can be difficult and virtually impossible to control to demand, although making changes to the other systems will help);
- how you *behave* (the easiest thing to change when we are feeling low).

To change your behavior, start by getting some idea of how your activities are connected to your mood. You can do this by recognizing the amount of pleasure and the sense of achievement you get from the activity. To do this you will need to complete an *activity diary*. This is similar to the hourly diary described on page 73. Each hour of the day you write down what you were doing (your activity) and how you were feeling (your mood). Next you rate how much pleasure you were getting from your activity and the degree to which you felt any sense of achievement. Rate pleasure and achievement from 0–100 per cent, with 0 meaning none at all and 100 meaning the most possible. Complete the blank version on page 132 to get some idea of where you are at now. Once you've established your current level or baseline of activity, you can then schedule in more activities that give you a sense of both pleasure and achievement. Have a look at the example below. This will help you complete one yourself for every day of the week. What does the example mean to you? What patterns can you see?

You'll see from this example that there is clearly a link between what we do and our mood. Having lunch with a

TABLE 6.18: EXAMPLE OF ONE DAY FROM A WEEKLY ACTIVITY DIARY

Time	Activity	Mood	Pleasure	Achievement
9–10 a.m.	Watching TV, thinking about things	Bored, tearful, anxious	10%	0%
10–11 a.m.	Watching TV	Bored	0%	0%
11–12 p.m.	Getting ready to meet a friend	Anxious	30%	50%
12–2 p.m.	Lunch with friend	Cheerful	60%	80%
2–3 p.m.	Sitting at home	Lonely	0%	0%
3–5 p.m.	Reading a book	Angry, unable to concentrate	0%	0%
5–7 p.m.	Asleep	Tired	0%	0%
7–10 p.m.	Watching TV	Bored	10%	0%

friend brought the most positive mood, and also gave the greatest sense of achievement for that day. Often when you're doing one activity, such as watching television you may also be going over things in your mind. Be aware of these thoughts and record them in your thought record. Again, notice when you're doing things that seem to give you little pleasure. It may be that the situation or activity provokes such anxiety that any sense of pleasure is lost or diminished.

Once you've completed your own activity diary (using Table 6.19 overleaf) for one week, you'll be able to look back over your ratings and ask yourself a series of questions:

- Did my mood change over the week? If so, from what to what?
- Was there a link between the things I did and how I felt?
- What activities give me pleasure and/or a sense of achievement?
- Are there certain days, times or situations that make my mood better or worse?
- Are there themes or patterns that I have only just become aware of?
- What are the sorts of activities I can increase because they make me feel better and decrease because they make me feel worse?

As you begin to address these questions, a plan of action may become clearer. The key to success at this level is to *turn each activity into an experiment*. Don't avoid an activity because you think you won't enjoy it. Invariably it's the negative thought patterns or the cognitive errors that are

TABLE 6.19: BLANK DAY FROM A WEEKLY ACTIVITY DIARY

Day and Date:

Time	Activity	Mood	Pleasure	Achievement
6–7 a.m.				
7–8 a.m.				
8–9 a.m.				
9–10 a.m.				
10–11 a.m.				
11–12 p.m.				
12–1 p.m.				
1–2 p.m.				
2–3 p.m.				
3–4 p.m.				
4–5 p.m.				
5–6 p.m.				
6–7 p.m.				
7–8 p.m.				
8–9 p.m.				
9–10 p.m.				
10–11 p.m.				
11–12 a.m.				

making you feel anxious and stopping you from doing something. Complete a thought record both *before* you do something and *after* the event. Now compare how you predicted it would go, and how much pleasure and achievement you thought you'd get, with how it actually went by completing the same ratings. If they're the same, try again but think about the feelings you had before the activity and how they might have influenced the final outcome. For example, if you believed that you wouldn't enjoy going to the pub with your friends because your DPAFU would be worse in a confined space and smoky atmosphere, the chances are that you'd be right as you would have paid so much attention to the atmosphere, your feelings of DPAFU and how right you were that you wouldn't enjoy the activity. You'd fail to notice the positive aspects, such as being with your friends. It's also worth reading through the section on managing anxiety. This will help you see whether anticipating events, or ruminating on them, lowers your mood.

It is clear from talking to people who suffer with DPAFU that they do begin to avoid social situations and being with other people. To start with, this can be in very subtle ways. Eventually though you can end up avoiding other people as much as possible. People often explain that they feel unconnected to, or unreal around, other people. They may also worry that people will think they're somehow odd. Social isolation affects mood in a number of ways: lowering your mood and reducing your self-esteem and/or self-confidence. Not being around people also confirms your belief that you are 'odd' and that others will see that there is something wrong with you. It also reinforces your disconnectedness from others. Again, these ideas become a negative and circular argument.

You can apply the same strategies to low mood or depression as you do to your DPAFU. First, identify all the things you believe that DPAFU sensations stop you from doing and

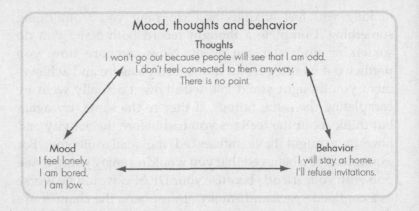

the things it makes you do more of. Then think about how much pleasure, stress, distress or satisfaction each one gives you. It may seem obvious that you wouldn't want to repeat the things that made you feel bad, but what about the things you used to enjoy and/or gave you a positive feeling? An example might be going to the cinema. Maybe you've stopped going because it made some of the sensations associated with DPAFU worse. But this may have been at the expense of going out with a good friend on a regular basis. Begin to schedule these activities back into your life gradually. But be careful not to overdo things all at once; this may leave you feeling exhausted or overwhelmed.

When you begin to recognize how you're feeling, you can begin to link the thoughts, feelings and behaviors that accompany each mood and you'll begin to notice the impact your thought patterns have on your mood and behavior.

Recognizing change and preventing relapse

People often feel disappointed that progress in overcoming their DPAFU isn't as quick as they'd hoped. But bear in mind that, for most people, DPAFU is a long-standing condition that may have developed over a number of years (see Alexi's story on page 19). And though it's very likely that eventually you'll feel better, it's not surprising that it takes time to make progress.

It can also sometimes be hard to see that there's been a change in your DPAFU. This is why the use of diaries or record sheets is invaluable. When you look back, you'll often find that change *has* taken place, though it may have been slow and gradual. Often people have different ideas about what constitutes change. For example, one man started treatment after many years of being unemployed and living at home with his parents. He always reported that 'nothing had changed, and everything was just the same'. This was despite now having a new girlfriend, doing voluntary work three days per week and living with friends. On the other hand, one woman reported being 'cured' although everything else in her life remained constant. She was still unable to do the same things as before. She just felt better.

For these reasons it's important that you keep your *goals* in mind and ensure they follow the SMART rules so that you can measure change. You also need to ask yourself whether, if you didn't have DPAFU, you'd still have these problems. Would you still feel low or anxious at times? And would your relationships be any more successful? The chances are that some problems will still remain. We all come up against a wide variety of problems and difficulties in life. It's part of the human condition to try to make sense of what is happening to us. That's why it's very easy sometimes to blame one thing on another. Research has shown that there is a tendency to attribute all physical and emotional sensations to DPAFU. There may be no good reason to think this except that it feels like this is the case. This is the cognitive error of *emotional reasoning*.

If, after working through this book, you still feel that you've not made any progress, or you've had a setback, you could either go along to your GP and ask to be referred to a therapist or try working through the book again. But remember that it is not uncommon to make progress in short bursts. For some, progress may be slow to start; others reach a plateau and feel there is little point in continuing with treatment.

Be aware of the following factors that may contribute towards you feeling that you are either 'stuck' or having a 'relapse'. After all, forewarned is forearmed.

- Spending increasing amounts of time focusing on how you are feeling and what is happening to your DPAFU can make you much more aware of your feelings and can make it seem as if things are getting worse.
- Stressful life events such as bereavement, moving home, beginning or ending a relationship or starting a new job will still happen. Don't blame all your negative feelings on DPAFU.
- Feeling low or depressed may not be connected to DPAFU.
- Physical illness can leave you feeling emotionally as well as physically drained.
- Using illicit drugs or excessive alcohol as a coping strategy will almost certainly make you feel a bit 'spacey' and detached, and will worsen your DPAFU. The side- or after-effects of such substances may also increase low mood and/or anxiety.

If you do find yourself having a setback that is more than the usual fluctuation in health and well-being that we all experience, don't panic! Instead think what has been happening. Is this setback a response to an event or situation? If so, think about revisiting the sections on managing stress, problem-solving and relaxation. If the setback feels as if it has come out of the blue, use thought records to try to pinpoint the context in which it arose. What do you think the setback means? Are you worrying about DPAFU? Are you noticing more symptoms? You may want to revisit the psychological model on page 35 and see how what is happening to you fits. If you feel that your mood is becoming lower and you're feeling more despondent, ask your GP for individual (face-to-face) therapy.

7

Other useful techniques

'Grounding' strategies

Some people who experience DPAFU do so because they have experienced traumatic events in their past (this might have been the case for Mina, who lost her mother to a terminal illness, see page 17). These traumas could have happened in childhood and/or adulthood. Some traumatic events can happen at any age, such as being in a life-threatening situation, for example a natural disaster or road traffic accident, witnessing violence or death, experiencing a physical attack, or suffering a serious illness. Childhood traumas may include emotional, physical or sexual abuse, as well as neglect or bullying. Not surprisingly, all of these extremely stressful experiences can lead to significant emotional difficulties in the months or years following. This book isn't specifically targeted at helping you recover from trauma. If you are suffering major impairment to your well-being and ability to function as a result of such traumas, it's best if you seek professional help, starting with your GP. Again, CBT can be a highly effective treatment. However, there are also some excellent self-help guides, such as *Overcoming Childhood Trauma* by Helen Kennerley and *Overcoming Traumatic Stress* by Claudia Herbert and Ann Wetmore, which can offer strategies and guidance (see the section on further reading on page 225). Even if you haven't experienced the kind of trauma described, you may find the following techniques very helpful in combating your DPAFU.

Childhood traumas often lead to DPAFU or other types of *dissociative* experiences in which we become detached from reality. Usually this is because a child cannot physically escape from a situation that is frightening or abusive. All too often they are helpless to defend themselves and can only escape using the power of their mind to mentally detach themselves from the situation. For some people this detachment appears to come automatically; for others it is something that they learn to do over time. Types of dissociation may include having *out of body experiences* (where it feels as though you have left your body but are able to watch what is happening from a distance), self-hypnosis or using imaginary places to which to escape. Experiencing DPAFU can be one of the strategies used to 'cut-off' or detach. In adult traumas too, the same types of dissociative experiences, including DPAFU, can occur at the time of the trauma and afterwards.

If you've experienced trauma in childhood and/or adulthood, and had DPAFU or any other type of dissociation at the time, it's possible that these sensations will reoccur if you're reminded of your trauma in some way. These reminders don't have to be very precise; sometimes the DPAFU can be set off by the vaguest of triggers, such as a specific smell, a particular word, a place or someone who has a similar appearance to your abuser. Suddenly, you can be overwhelmed with DPAFU. You may even feel as if you are back in the traumatic situation again, almost as though you are reliving the emotions and sensations you felt at the time. Understandably, this is very distressing and frightening.

If this is your experience of DPAFU, don't despair; there are some helpful techniques to combat it. These techniques are commonly called *grounding strategies*. They are so named because they aim to 'ground' you in the here and now, in the present time and place, rather than in the past trauma. Grounding strategies take several forms, using your surroundings, words or statements, images, posture or objects, and we discuss them all in the following pages. Read through this section and try out each of the grounding strategies to see which ones work best for you. You will need to keep practising with each of these, ideally for a few minutes every day, to make them effective. Start off when you feel relatively relaxed and you have no DPAFU or your DPAFU is not too severe. Then, once you've gained some control over your DPAFU, you can use these techniques to help you when the DPAFU is worse.

Using your surroundings to ground yourself

Look around at your surroundings. Try to notice everything in the most precise detail possible and describe it to yourself. This is best done aloud if you can; otherwise do it silently in your head. Describe your surroundings using all five senses by asking yourself questions such as:

- Where am I right now? What town am I in? What building am I in? What day is it? What time is it?
- What do I see around me?
- What colours are there?
- What shapes can I see?
- What textures do I see around me?
- How bright or dark is it where I am?
- Can I hear anything and, if so, what exactly?
- What sensations do I feel on my body? Can I feel the seat I am sitting on? Can I feel the ground under my feet? Can I feel the air on my skin?

- Is there anything I can smell? What sort of smell is this?
- Can I taste anything?

Keep asking yourself these questions until you feel fully grounded in time, place and reality.

Grounding words or statements

Some people find the use of grounding words or positive statements very helpful. These should aim to make you feel strong, positive and acutely aware of being alive in the moment. Remind yourself of your good qualities, your strengths or the good things in your life. Examples of positive grounding statements might be:

- I am strong and I will get through this.
- I will succeed if I keep trying.
- My family and friends are here to support me.
- These feelings will pass.
- I will make the most of today.
- I am here and I am okay.

Create a list of words or statements that make you feel positive and grounded. Write these on cards that you can carry around with you so that you can read them to yourself when you start to experience DPAFU.

Grounding images

If you feel overwhelmed by your DPAFU (or any other negative feelings), using visual imagery can be very calming and grounding. Think of a place that brings you a sense of peace and tranquillity. This can be a real place that you know (such as a beach, park or building) or an imaginary place, like a fantasy castle, or floating on a cloud. If it's a real place, choose somewhere that has no negative memories associated with it. Shut your eyes and imagine yourself in your 'special place'. Take the time to really focus on the details of your surroundings; the more detail you can create, the greater your sense of grounding will be. What do you see around you? Are you on your own or would you like someone to be there with you? Who would that person be? Would you like a favourite pet or animal to keep you company and/or protect you? What are you doing in your special place? What can you hear? If you're outside, can you hear the sounds of nature? If other people are around, are they talking or laughing? Is it warm or cold where you are? Can you feel any particular sensations on your body? What smells or tastes do you associate with this place? What emotions do you experience when you imagine yourself here? Where do you feel those emotions in your body? What single word would sum up this special place for you?

Practise your grounding image every day. Try to add more detail each time so that it becomes more and more vivid. The greater the detail and realism, the greater will be your sense of security, calmness and grounding when you visualize it.

Grounding posture

You may find it helpful to change your physical position if you start to experience DPAFU. Adopting a stance that makes you feel strong and grounded will work best for you. This may be standing up straight, with shoulders back and head held high. It may involve consciously letting go of any tension you feel in your body, keeping your shoulders from hunching and letting your arms and hands relax by your side. Alternatively, you might prefer settling into a comfortable chair and allowing yourself to flop like a rag doll to relieve the feelings of tension. Perhaps stretching to the sky or becoming aware of the weight of your feet on the ground will help to ground you. Try several different postures to see what works best for you.

Grounding objects

Objects can be useful for giving a sense of grounding and bringing you back to reality. Choose something that has personal significance for you, and that you can carry on your person or have to hand. Examples might be a piece of jewellery, your keys and key ring, a pen, a scarf, a handkerchief, a soft toy, a photo, a small bottle of your favourite perfume, your business card or a letter. Any of these could work. When you start to feel sensations of DPAFU use your grounding object to remind you of who you are and where you are.

Grounding tips

In order for your strategies to work, you'll need to practise them regularly. The beauty of grounding techniques is that they are so easy to do, anywhere and at any time. You can close your eyes and use your grounding image while sitting on a bus, hold your grounding object when in a meeting, adopt your grounding posture when in social situations, use your grounding words when you wake up in the morning. In fact, you can ground yourself in your surroundings at any time of the day or night. Practise the strategies before you need them and you'll find they work better when you do! One word of caution: don't use these techniques as an excuse for avoiding some situation that, though stressful, is important for you to see through. In other words, don't let grounding (or indeed any other technique) become just another safety behavior (see pages 33–34).

Problem solving

The ground we cover in this section isn't specific to DPAFU. Instead, we're going to show you an approach that's useful when trying to solve certain types of problems, such as when you encounter a dilemma or when you're unsure of the best option to choose.

Step 1: Clearly define the problem. What are your choices or options? This may involve drawing up a list and writing things down. As in the previous exercises, you will need to be very specific. How will you know when the problem is resolved? How will you measure any change? Possible problem areas include: intimate relationships; family relationships; friendships; employment or study; money and debt; housing; legal matters; substance dependency; physical or mental health; sexual orientation; and bereavement or impending loss. Once you have the problem well-defined, you'll be able to set your goals.

Step 2: Think of as many answers or solutions as possible. At this stage, it doesn't matter how unlikely or impossible these solutions may seem. One of the main reasons that people find it difficult to successfully solve their problems is that they're too dismissive of possible solutions. If you hear yourself starting to say 'Yes, but . . .', stop! Write your suggestion down anyway. Sometimes unrealistic solutions help you think more laterally and they can help to generate good solutions. You may also wish to survey the advice and opinions of other people and ask them what they would do in the same situation. Once you have a long list of possible solutions, you need to evaluate each of these in turn. Write out a list of pros and cons for solutions that seem most likely. What are the advantages and disadvantages of one option over another? What are the advantages and disadvantages of *not* choosing one option over another? Although these questions sound remarkably similar, they don't always generate the same responses. For example, imagine that you are thinking about ending a relationship. What would be the advantages and disadvantages of leaving? What would be the advantages and disadvantages of staying?

Step 3: Identify your own resources, skills and abilities, and think about how you've coped in the past. What worked well and what didn't work? Do you use avoidance or unhelpful coping methods like alcohol or drugs? What impact do these methods of coping have on your problems? Who are you able to share your problems with? Do you have friends or family members that you can discuss your problems with? Remember the old adage: 'a problem shared is a problem halved'.

Step 4: Once you've written down the most viable options, choose one to try out first. Work out in detail the steps you'll have to take, the order you'll need to take them in, and the time frame for each. The better your planning at this stage, the more likely you are to be successful. These steps might include rehearsing in your imagination what you're going to say or do. This will help build your confidence when you think through the likely consequences. You could also role-play the scene with a friend or family member. If your problem is more to do with time management, you might find an activity diary helpful. For example, if you've got behind in your studies or work, plan to add just 30 minutes more each day. By the end of the week you will have achieved three and a half hours additional work or study. If on the other hand your problem is more one of unhelpful beliefs, you may wish to use a thought record. As we discussed earlier, you can then challenge these beliefs. For certain problems, you may also wish to obtain expert advice from organizations such as the Citizens Advice Bureau, Shelter, Mind, or from a solicitor or local law centre.

Step 5: Carry out the solution. Go ahead and do what you've planned.

Step 6: Evaluate the outcome. This may be in the form of a daily or weekly diary and it'll depend on the goals you identified at the beginning of the problem-solving exercise. For example, you may wish to rate the problem as solved, good progress, some progress or no change. Common causes of difficulty with problem-solving include low self-esteem or lack of self-confidence. Or it may be that the problems selected represent long-standing personal difficulties, such as a long history of very poor or dysfunctional relationships. In these cases more traditional face-to-face therapy will be needed. If your outcome has not been as good as you'd like, you may want to return to your brainstorming list and choose the next most viable solution. Go through steps 3–6 again with this solution. Evaluate your outcome again. Did this work better?

This six-step approach can be helpful for many types of problem, for example relationship difficulties, including ending intimate partner relationships and falling out with friends or family; whether to leave a job or change roles within employment; study problems such as falling behind with coursework or failing exams; time management;

problems bringing up your children; and indeed any other major choices that we face in day-to-day life. Remember some situations cannot change – you may, for example, have suffered bereavement, lost your job or been diagnosed with cancer. Problem solving is about saying: Okay, there are some things I can't change, but I still have lots of options open to me as to what I do next. How can I choose the best option? How can I take the first steps?

Relaxation and mindfulness

Many people who suffer with DPAFU believe that certain forms of relaxation make their DPAFU seem worse. Indeed some cases have been described that actually followed deep meditation. It is possible that the sense of being detached from the hustle and bustle of what's going on around us is a bit unnerving for some people and they can be afraid of 'losing themselves'. However, if you are one of those people who feels depersonalized when worries and anxieties have been building up, it is unlikely that relaxation itself will make DPAFU seem worse. Instead, it is more likely that having the time and space to relax heightens your awareness of how you're feeling. When you're relaxing there's little to distract you and so there is a tendency to focus on yourself. As we saw in the psychological model outlined in Figure 4.5 (see page 35), the more you notice and look for sensations, the more you'll find. But even if you have found that relaxation has made your DPAFU worse in the past, it's very important that you don't avoid relaxation altogether. Relaxation won't in itself make your DPAFU worse. We all need to relax and, in fact, not allowing yourself to do so may lead to additional problems such as stress and anxiety. Now that you have a greater understanding of how your thoughts and behaviors can impact on your DPAFU, have another go at relaxation with Exercise 1 on page 149. Perhaps this time, if you realize that it wasn't the relaxation, but rather your heightened self-monitoring that made you more aware of your sensations, you'll have a more positive experience.

Relaxation comes in a variety of guises. You could try exercise, such as yoga, swimming or a good aerobic workout. You might prefer to spend some time on a favourite hobby. Or you might find that you have most success with relaxation tapes and/or meditation. Experiment to see what works best for you. It might be an activity not traditionally associated with relaxation, such as gardening, cooking, sewing or DIY.

If you find that you avoid relaxation because you believe it makes your DPAFU seem worse, you'll need to tackle this problem. Try to identify what it is about relaxation that you don't like. Perhaps you find that memories or images of past traumatic events come into your mind when you try to relax. But because relaxation is so important this needs to be addressed. In the same way as you used thought records to write down, examine, challenge and alter your ideas and beliefs, you can do exactly the same again here. (You might find it helpful to refer back to the section on thought records on page 96 to refresh your memory.) Briefly, the idea is to allow the thoughts you have to come into your head and make a mental note of any ideas and themes that keep occurring. Once your relaxation session has finished, write them down in your thought record and begin to challenge them like you did before.

One very effective type of relaxation is called *mindfulness*. It's a form of meditation that is increasingly being applied to a variety of psychological problems, and it was developed by Jon Kabat-Zinn and John Teasdale. Mindfulness has proved valuable in treating depression and anxiety, which usually involve rumination and worry. The aim of the therapy is to observe the processing that is going on in your mind while you're worrying or mulling over thoughts. Through a variety of exercises, including yoga-like positions, breathing and concentration, you allow whatever thoughts you have to come into your mind. You don't try to stop or change them; instead, you simply allow them to come. You 'watch' them appear, disappear and reappear. Most importantly, you try not to become attached to them or engage with them. Increasingly, you become aware that you are not your thoughts. They occur because you generate them, but they're simply mental events and aren't necessarily true. In all areas of life we can sometimes make mistakes, and the same is true for our thoughts, ideas, beliefs, images and feelings.

EXERCISE 1

Progressive relaxation

Start by either sitting or lying in a quiet, comfortable room. Make sure you won't be disturbed and that there are no distractions. Close your eyes and become aware of your own breath. Try to breathe normally and avoid either shallow breathing or breathing too deeply. During this exercise, you'll focus your attention on each part of your body in turn and notice how it feels. You may find it easier to start at your toes and feet and move up your legs to the genital region, then the abdomen, back, chest, arms, hands, fingers, neck and head. Alternatively, find the order that makes the most sense to you. While you focus on each area, breathe in and notice the difference between tension and relaxation. Then, as you breathe out, visualize that part of your body relaxing and letting go of all the tension in the muscles. During the relaxation, try to just *be*. Allow any thoughts to come, rather than fighting them. Instead just try to observe and be aware of them. After all, they're just thoughts. You can't make your DPAFU worse just by thinking about it, even though you may feel that you can. All that might happen is that you become more aware of the sensations associated with DPAFU. But let these thoughts and sensations come and try not to e frightened. You can't cause a brain tumour, schizophrenia or any form of madness just by thinking about it. Remember the psychological model we presented in Part 1 (see page 35) and, if you feel the DPAFU more strongly, don't try to avoid it or distract yourself.

By adopting this position, you'll learn to accept negative thoughts, ideas and emotions. You'll see that the sensations of DPAFU are nothing more than mental events, rather than believing they're predictions of inevitable disaster. You'll become less frightened and distressed, and you'll find it easier to turn your attention to the here and now. You'll live in the present, rather than ruminating over what went wrong, how it went wrong, and what you could or should have done differently. Going over and over the same things only leads to you feeling worse; it doesn't lead to answers.

If you want to learn mindfulness techniques, we recommend that you attend a recognized training course, which will last about eight weeks. There are several centres around the UK that offer such training but many local Buddhist centres also do the same. If you can't get to one of the courses, you can practise daily on your own. Start out by practising for between 15–30 minutes and build up to 60–90 minutes. You'll find lots of books and audio tapes or CDs to help you develop mindfulness skills, and we've included a brief exercise on pages 151–152 for you to try out on your own.

Relaxation and mindfulness tips

You may find it helpful to tape-record some instructions to remind yourself to breathe steadily and where to focus your attention. Play these instructions while you try out the exercises. Alternatively, you may wish to buy a relaxation tape to help you. Tapes that contain some guided imagery are especially good. Or you can add on time for your grounding image to the end of the relaxation or mindfulness exercise.

EXERCISE 2

Mindfulness

Start by sitting in a quiet, comfortable room. You can lie down if you prefer although this is more likely to make you feel sleepy, which is not the goal of mindfulness. Make sure you won't be disturbed and that there are no distractions. Close your eyes and become aware of your own breath. Try to breathe normally and avoid either shallow breathing or breathing too deeply. Next imagine that the breath you take in is in soothing colours such as blues or greens. Imagine this clean, fresh, soothing breath travelling and circulating all around your body.

Next imagine that the breath you breathe out is red or black and is ridding yourself of anger, toxins, negativity (or whatever feels more suitable for you). Continue to do this for a bit and after a while begin to just focus on the 'in' and 'out' breath. You may find it useful to count each 'out' breath until you reach 21, and then start again. Don't try to stop any thoughts that come to mind. Don't worry, or tell yourself off, if you find you're no longer concentrating on the task. You may find that you have drifted off and followed a train of thought. This is actually very likely, and if it happens, don't judge yourself or feel you're doing the exercise wrongly. The idea is to simply become aware that this has happened and then bring yourself back to observing the breath.

Different thoughts and feelings will arise and your task is to simply observe them. Don't criticize yourself if you find that you're distracted by things such as noises outside the room. Each time you notice that your mind has wandered off, just calmly guide it back again to watching your breath.

Initially, try to do this exercise for 10–15 minutes at a time. Sometimes when you sit down to do this, you'll find your mind is very agitated and other times you'll feel it is dull and lethargic. Try not to get frustrated by this and instead just continue observing the breath. Gradually, after doing this exercise for a while, you will find there are times when the mind starts to quieten and you will begin to feel a sense of peace and calmness.

At the end of your mindfulness sessions, record the thoughts, ideas, images or themes that popped into your mind. Try to build up a profile over a few days (up to a week). Are the thoughts very similar? Are there just a few things that you regularly dwell on? Once you've done this, try to challenge the ideas using thought records as suggested in previous sections. You may also want to use some of the strategies we discussed in the previous sections on anxiety, low mood and problem solving.

If you've had difficult experiences in the past during relaxation-type exercises, you might be worried that your DPAFU might worsen. Or perhaps you're concerned that you might get feelings of panic. If so, remind yourself to think of yourself as a scientist carrying out an experiment. Scientists start by predicting what might happen in an experiment. The prediction here would be that nothing catastrophic will happen. If you do begin to feel panicky, remind yourself that it is just anxiety. If you're anxious, your heart rate is increased, but that doesn't mean you're going to have a heart attack. Your breathing rate will increase, but that doesn't mean you're going to suffocate. When you increase your breathing, your mouth goes dry. When you're feeling anxious, your blood flow is concentrated between the heart and the brain, which may lead to your hands, feet and limbs feeling tingly or very heavy or numb, or to you experiencing pins and needles. These are the physical reasons why you're having these sensations. When you know what to expect, and what follows in the chain reaction, you'll feel less scared if it happens.

Mindfulness has a long history as a means of promoting good mental health, but it's only recently been brought into psychological therapies. There isn't enough research on DPAFU to say whether the techniques suggested in this section really will help you. Some people will prefer the grounding approach. But if mindfulness and relaxation seem right for you, give them a try.

Exercise, diet and sleep

Exercise

There are no specific physical exercises that will help with your DPAFU, but there is a vast body of research that indicates that any physical, oxygen-burning exercise (i.e. anything that gets you out of breath) helps improve low mood, anxiety and stress. Exercise need not be expensive and you don't need to join a gym. You can cycle, walk and run almost anywhere and they're either free or relatively cheap. Local authority leisure facilities often offer reduced rates for off-peak times and/or concessionary rates. Many GPs prescribe physical exercise as a treatment for anxiety or depression, and these 'exercise referral schemes' also offer discounted rates. Many people who suffer with DPAFU report feeling better following a good workout and find swimming very relaxing. Sports where you need to concentrate hard (e.g. racquet or ball sports) will also be helpful in keeping your focus on your environment and giving your mind a break from worry and rumination. Try a variety of forms of exercise to see what works best for you.

Diet

People with DPAFU sensations don't need to follow any specific diet or avoid any particular foods. In fact, people who suffer with DPAFU are like most other people; they report that when they're feeling less than 100 per cent they have a greater need to eat a healthy diet including more fresh fruit, vegetables and fibre and to reduce the amount of sugar, salt and fats they consume. Of the 400 people who have participated in research at our Unit, there is no general consensus regarding diet. However, caffeine is a stimulant and in excess can mimic symptoms of anxiety. So if you experience anxiety in any form, reducing your caffeine intake may be helpful. Remember that caffeine comes in many guises; it's in cola-type soft drinks and many 'energy boosting' drinks, as well as the more obvious coffee and non-herbal tea.

Sleep

As we all know, poor sleep can leave you feeling exhausted the next day. In turn, you're more likely to feel 'spaced out' and/or 'disconnected'. You may also find that your ability to concentrate is diminished. All of these sensations are very similar to DPAFU and you may have noticed that when you're tired your DPAFU seems worse. Poor sleep patterns can lead to negative cycles of behavior. You wake up feeling tired so you have an afternoon nap; then you find it difficult to go to sleep at night. You lie in bed worrying about not getting to sleep, eventually dropping off in the early hours of the morning, only to get up again feeling tired – and so the problem continues.

Although the use of prescribed sleeping pills can work well in the short term for most people, their effectiveness can diminish very quickly. All too often in the past the dose was increased and increased until soon people were unable to sleep without taking a pill. Today GPs are less likely to prescribe them for the longer term because a vast amount of research has shown the risks of dependence with this type of medication. Generally people are encouraged to seek out more natural methods to improve their sleep. Luckily, there has been a lot of research in this area and some very effective techniques are around. There are self-help guides too that specifically address this problem, for example *Overcoming Insomnia and Sleep Problems* by Colin Espie.

If you're having problems sleeping, you may find the following suggestions useful. However, you may need to put these into practice over a number of weeks before you see the benefits. Please don't feel too disheartened if your sleep pattern does not right itself immediately. The key to success is not to give up and to give it at least two to four weeks to reset your sleep pattern. The only long-term remedy for poor sleep is to get into a positive cycle through a process of *sleep hygiene*. Here are some of the golden rules:

- **Don't go to bed until you feel sleepy.** Don't go to bed just because it's 'bedtime' or you're bored. Stay up until you're tired, no matter how late this may be. Prepare yourself for sleep by having a warm bath or reading a relaxing book. Don't do anything remotely stimulating for at least an hour before bed, and don't have any caffeine-based drinks (tea, coffee, chocolate, Coca-Cola) for at least two hours before bed. Over a few weeks, gradually limit your caffeine intake during the day. Avoid alcohol and nicotine for several hours before bed. Alcohol may make you feel that you can get to sleep quicker, but that sleep is likely to be of poor quality. You'll wake up feeling tired and suffering the side effects of alcohol!
- **Your bedroom is for sleeping only.** Don't associate the bedroom with anything else. Try not to use your bedroom during the day. Don't lie in bed and watch TV, listen to the radio or read, no matter how relaxing these things are. It's okay to do these things if you don't have a sleep problem, but when you suffer from insomnia you need to be strict about the activities you

do in the bedroom. Instead, do these activities downstairs or in another room to help induce sleepiness. Sex is the only exception. Sex may help you to feel sleepy – especially if it's at night.

- **If you're not asleep within 15 minutes, get back up.** You don't want to associate your bedroom and your bed with lying awake. When we lie in bed awake, we often find our mind becomes preoccupied with all sorts of thoughts and worries. This can often leave us feeling more anxious, depressed or stressed. So when you get into bed to sleep, turn out all the lights. If you're not asleep within 15 minutes, get up again and go somewhere else. Keep warm and do something quiet and not stimulating. This is a good time to try your relaxation, mindfulness or grounding image exercises. Or you could do something very boring instead such as the ironing or doing a job you've been putting off. Don't drink, eat or smoke (smoking is a mild stimulant). Avoid associating this time with anything meaningful or pleasant. Only go back to bed when you feel sleepy. If you're not asleep within 15 minutes, get up and repeat this sequence – all through the night if you have to. It might seem better to just keep lying in bed, rather than getting up every 15 minutes. However, research shows that the 15 minute rule will work if you stick with it – and normally within a few nights.

- **Get up at the same time each morning.** This applies even if you only managed one hour's sleep. Set an alarm and get up when it goes off. It's important to establish a routine. You shouldn't get up later than 9 a.m., even if you don't have anything to do that day. Don't make any exceptions – even for the weekend – when you first start.

- **Don't sleep during the day.** Stick to this rule no matter how tired you are. Don't try to catch up on sleep; this will spoil all your hard work. If you find yourself feeling sleepy during the afternoons, go out for a walk, do some housework, or phone a friend instead. Don't go to bed or nap on the sofa. If you need to re-energize yourself during the day, try taking several deep breaths of fresh air.
- **If you sleep too much, gradually bring the time that you usually get up forward by one hour per week.** If, say, you're sleeping until 1 p.m., then in week one set your alarm for 12 noon, and in week two set it for 11 a.m. Do this until you're getting up no later than 9 a.m.

A word of warning! Be aware that you may feel worse and more tired when you first use these strategies. But don't give up. Rest assured that it may take a couple of weeks to break many years of poor sleep habits but it is definitely worth persevering.

8

How to deal with problems related to DPAFU

Low self-esteem and self-confidence

Self-esteem and self-confidence are concepts that are often used interchangeably. They simply refer to how you feel about yourself, including your sense of self-worth, your belief in yourself and/or your abilities, and the judgements you make about yourself. Improving or being satisfied with these areas of your life can be difficult and may be worth addressing in their own right, especially since problems with self-esteem are often deep-seated and may have been with you since you were young. Again there's a wide selection of books on this subject, including a few good self-help guides such as Melanie Fennell's *Overcoming Low Self-Esteem* and David Burns's *10 Days to Great Self-Esteem*. We don't look at this issue in any depth, because it's not a major feature associated with DPAFU. However, since some people with DPAFU also have low self-esteem or lack self-confidence and this can have an impact on their DPAFU, we cover how this can be self-managed using the same principles already outlined.

First, as with all psychological difficulties, before you start you need to clearly define the problem. It's not enough to say you have low self-esteem; you need to think how that low self-esteem impacts upon your life. For example, you may feel that you can't speak up at meetings because you'll say the wrong thing or make a fool of yourself. Part of the problem of course could be that, because DPAFU makes you feel 'odd', you don't want to draw further attention to yourself. Or it may be that you don't believe in your own abilities or knowledge. Again, once you've defined the problem, you need to decide how you would like things to be different. This involves thinking about the changes you would like to make. You can then set goals to help you make those changes – and remember that your goals need to follow the SMART rules that we discussed earlier (see page 67). Once you've done this, you can move on to the next part of the process.

Using thought records, try to become aware of your thoughts in the situations you've identified as problematic. You need to examine these thoughts closely and look out for any cognitive errors (see page 42). Again, examine the evidence that supports and refutes your beliefs. Can you think of any alternative explanations for how you're thinking, feeling and behaving?

Another helpful strategy is to carry out surveys among supportive friends and family to see how valid your ideas really are. You could do this by way of a light-hearted game in which you ask them to list your top five qualities or attributes. You might want to predict what they'll say and compare notes afterwards. Everyone who tries this exercise is pleasantly surprised by the responses they receive. An example from Alexi is given overleaf.

Alexi described himself as 'quiet, solitary and a bit boring', but his friends and work colleagues saw him very differently as being friendly, thoughtful and reliable. What he saw as negative qualities, they saw in a positive light. If you believe that you possess many negative or neutral qualities, it's easy to see how you can easily end up feeling low or bad about

TABLE 8.1: A LIST OF TOP 5 QUALITIES/ATTRIBUTES		
	Predicted attribute	Actual attribute
1	Quiet	Friendly
2	Solitary	Thoughtful
3	Pushover	Honest
4	Boring	Reliable
5	Non-confrontational	Trustworthy

yourself. That's why it's important to challenge your self-perceptions by comparing them with other people's views.

Often people talk about self-esteem as though it's just about one thing, and people rate themselves without really thinking about what it means. But usually someone's self-esteem is made up of lots of different qualities. So another way of trying to increase your self-esteem is to use the *continuum method*. First, give your self-worth a rating from 0–100 per cent, where 0 means that you're not at all a worthwhile person, and 100 means that you're a totally worthwhile person. Write this rating down so you can refer to it later. Next, list all the factors that you think are important to making a person worthwhile. Try to think of as many qualities as possible, for example:

- Being successful at work.
- Having a good relationship.
- Being helpful to others.
- Having lots of friends.

The next step is to put these qualities on to a continuum. A continuum is a sliding scale with extreme points at either end. The ends are the 0 per cent and the 100 per cent points. Let's look at what the extreme points could be for the above qualities:

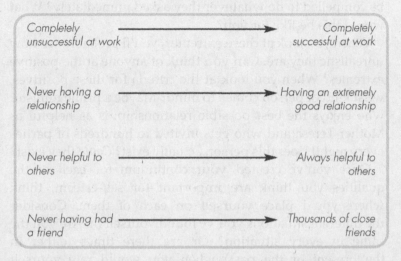

Completely unsuccessful at work ⟶ Completely successful at work

Never having a relationship ⟶ Having an extremely good relationship

Never helpful to others ⟶ Always helpful to others

Never having had a friend ⟶ Thousands of close friends

In terms of being successful at work, a score of 0 per cent would mean someone who has never had a job – perhaps someone who has never even had a job interview or indeed any response to a job application. On the other hand, what would being completely successful at work mean? What exactly does this mean for you? Would it be someone who is at the top of their profession and who has been for a very long time? Who comes to mind when you think of this? Perhaps someone like the US president, or someone who wins a Nobel Prize, might be considered in this way? Does it mean someone who has a very high income? If so, how much? Try to think of the extremes and who or what you're basing this on.

For helpfulness, one extreme might be never having helped anyone, never having offered anyone advice, never having loaned or given something to someone, or never having said something that made someone feel better if they were upset. Being 100 per cent helpful might mean that you help anyone who needs it, even if it creates a major problem for you. So, if someone asked you to help them, would you be compelled to do whatever they asked immediately? What would this be like for you?

When you look at these extremes, you'll probably see how unrealistic they are. Can you think of anyone at the positive extremes? When you look at the criteria for these positives, what kind of person comes to mind? Maybe a prime minister who enjoys the best possible relationship, is as helpful as Mother Teresa and who gets invited to hundreds of parties every night! Does this person actually exist? *Could* they exist?

Once you've created your continuum for each of the qualities you think are important for self-esteem, think where you'd place yourself on each of them. Consider the different situations you've found yourself in. Are you the same in every situation? Or are there times (either in the present or the past) when you would rate yourself differently? Have there been times or situations when other people may have rated you differently? Think back over your whole life, not just your recent difficulties. Give yourself a percentage rating for each of the qualities. Once you've done this, add up the total and divide by the number of qualities you listed in order to get your average score. How does this average compare to the rating for self-worth that you wrote down before you started this exercise? You'll probably find that the second rating is much higher. This is because when we think about self-esteem or self-worth we often don't stop to think about the qualities we are including in these concepts. When we do this, and then rate how we match up to the extremes, we often find that we are already much closer to being how we want to be than we think we are.

In the next step, begin to put together a series of positive statements about how you would like to see yourself. Write these sentences or statements on cards or small pieces of paper. Practise reading them out loud. Rate how much you believe each statement to be true. Keep a list of things that you do during the day that are examples of these positive statements; it's your daily self-esteem diary. Here's an example:

Positive belief: I am loveable

Examples of being loveable:

MONDAY

My daughter kissed me when she left for school.
My friend rang to invite me out.

TUESDAY

I helped my neighbour by getting her some shopping.
I went to work and did a good job.
I bought my daughter an ice cream.

WEDNESDAY

I sent a birthday card to a friend.
I listened to my colleague at work when she was upset.
My partner gave me a hug.

Think through all the small things that you've done during the day and jot them down. Regularly re-rate how much you believe the positive statement to be true. As you gather more evidence, you'll start to see your belief increase.

You can also be proactive in increasing your self-esteem. Think about what would have to happen before you'd believe a positive statement more strongly. Or what would have to happen for you not to believe something negative about yourself. Think about ways in which you could test out some of your beliefs and predictions about yourself. Begin to carry out your own experiments to test these beliefs and predictions. While you're carrying out these experiments, draw up a list of treats and rewards for yourself. These don't have to cost lots of money or take up lots of time. Rewards can range from a bar of chocolate, a trip to the local swimming pool or hairdressers, through to luxury spa weekends and overseas trips. Remember, it's good to treat yourself to whatever makes you feel good, whether that's pampering yourself, going to the gym, shopping or going to a football match. As they say in the advertisement, it's 'because you're worth it'!

If you constantly feel emotionally numb, low self-esteem and/or self-confidence may not be a problem for you. Just as nothing will make you feel good or better about yourself, nothing will make you feel bad or worse. So while the emotional numbness is a problem, low self-confidence or self-esteem won't be. If, on the other hand, you only feel negative emotions, you may want to go back and look over the section on managing low mood and anxiety.

Stress

There's nothing to suggest that people who suffer with DPAFU feel stress any more than others. If anything, you may even report feeling less stressed, possibly because you feel very little at all. It is often difficult to tease out what people mean when they say they feel stressed. We define stress *as the feeling of being under pressure, when you feel that the resources you have do not match up to what is required or demanded in any given situation.* In this section we discuss stress in general and not specifically in relation to DPAFU.

As ever, the first step is to identify the problem. This task may be made easier by keeping a *stress diary* over a week or two. At the end of each day, rate how stressed you have felt on a scale of, say, 0–10 or 0–100. Be clear about exactly what you're rating. Do you rate stress in terms of its severity during the day? Or in terms of how long it lasted? Or do you rate your stress levels in comparison to how you felt, say, three or four weeks ago? In fact, it really doesn't matter how you do it. What's most important is that you decide what you want to measure and be consistent. Once you have your rating, try to identify the factors you feel were responsible for, or contributed to, your stress. Have a look at the example below from Jay for an idea of how you might go about this task.

TABLE 8.2: EXAMPLE OF A COMPLETED STRESS DIARY		
Day	Rating	Factors causing or maintaining stress
Mon	30	Busy at work – things piling up because I was late.
Tue	70	Boss told me he wanted report by end of the day. Worried about it over lunch and found it hard to concentrate.
Wed	45	Took day off sick but I know there will be even more work tomorrow. Worrying about it at home.
Thurs	90	Loads of work to catch up on but I need to leave early to get some shopping. Friends are coming for dinner.
Fri	80	Busy trying to finish work. Dishes at home need washing from last night. All the housework to do.
Sat	10	Little stress since spent day in bed – although worrying a bit about the housework etc.
Sun	35	Worrying about work on Monday – spoiling my day.

Here is a blank copy for you to complete:

TABLE 8.3: BLANK STRESS DIARY		
Day	Rating	Factors causing or maintaining stress
Mon		
Tue		
Wed		
Thurs		
Fri		
Sat		
Sun		

Once you've monitored your stress levels over a week or two, you'll be able to identify the major *stressors* (the things that cause you stress) in your life. Of course, you may be more than aware of these already, in which case you won't need to complete the diary. In much the same way as you've done before, the key thing is to produce a well-defined description of the problem from which you can set your goals.

If we look back at Jay's example, he needs to decide if he's finding it hard to keep up with his workload because it's too big or because he doesn't manage his time well. If the workload is too big then his goal would be to reduce the load. He could speak to his line manager about what's reasonable and achievable in a working day. If, on the other hand, his stress is a result of poor time management, Jay's goal would be to improve this skill. A third option would be that the stress is a result of a combination of the two factors. It's important to be clear about contributory factors so that each one is managed or dealt with appropriately. There would be little point in Jay's manager reducing his workload if he continued to come in late and leave early in order to go shopping. While this might feel better in the short term, eventually Jay would find himself feeling stressed again.

Time management means just that. Managing your time in a more productive way. Start by examining how you spend your time over the day or the week. You can do this by using a form like the activity diary on page 132. Or better still you can devise your own record of how you spend your day. Once you've completed this for a few days, you'll be able to identify the times of the day that are particularly busy, and those where you have free time. Next, make a list of all the tasks, activities or chores that you would like to achieve over the day or the week. Remember to keep this list realistic. Take a blank activity diary sheet for each day and plan the day out, scheduling in the things you would like to do. Phase in one or two of these tasks gradually. Just like setting any goal, it'll help if you break it down into manageable chunks. If you try to take on too much too soon, you may end up not being able to complete all that you'd hoped. You might then use this as evidence that you are a 'failure', rather than the

TABLE 8.4: JAY'S ACTIVITY DIARY: MONDAY 4 JUNE	
Time	Activity
1–2 p.m.	Lunch chatting with friends. Late back to work – make it up at end of day
2–3 p.m.	Work
3–4 p.m.	Work
4–5 p.m.	Work
5–6 p.m.	Working late to make up for lost time
6–7 p.m.	Shopping on way home – late for collecting dry cleaning so no clothes for next day
7–8 p.m.	Cooking, eating and washing up
8–9 p.m.	TV
9–10 p.m.	TV
10–11 p.m.	Fell asleep on sofa
11–12 a.m.	Ironing clothes – exhausted

inevitable result of an unrealistic target. Have a look at the example for Jay above.

Once you have an idea of how you're spending your time, it'll be easier to prioritize those things you *need* to do and those that you *want* to do. You'll then be able to revise how you spend your time. Often you'll have to balance something pleasurable, like having lunch with friends, with a chore, like going shopping or doing the ironing. But a word of caution – don't use time management as an excuse to avoid certain important activities like socializing!

Here's Jay's list of the tasks he'd like to achieve on a Monday:

- Shopping.
- Collect dry cleaning from the weekend.
- Go to gym.

As you can see from Table 8.5 overleaf, Jay could achieve everything he wanted to with better time management. Giving up part of his lunch hour means he can do the shopping. He can then leave work on time, collect his dry cleaning and get to the gym. This leaves the evening for cooking, eating and relaxing in front of the TV without having to iron at midnight. Other time management tricks include cooking in bulk at the weekend, thus saving time in the week. Think about going to the gym or paying bills in your lunch hour. It's all about being more efficient, rather than doing more or less with your time!

One quick but effective solution to reduce stress is *exercise*. Various research studies have shown a link between increased exercise and decreased stress, anxiety and low mood (see page 153). Other quick-fix solutions might be to increase dedicated relaxation time (see page 150), or to talk to a trusted friend or family member. You could also use controlled breathing exercises, such as taking a slow and deep breath in through the nose to a count of two or four and out through the mouth to a count of four or eight. It doesn't matter what number you count to, just so long as the out breath is for twice the count of the in breath. The in breath will energize you, whereas the out breath is called the breath of relaxation. When you breathe in, try to fill your lungs so that your diaphragm is expanded. When you breathe out, try to expel all the air.

TABLE 8.5: JAY'S REVISED ACTIVITY DIARY: MONDAY 11 JUNE

Time	Activity
1–2 p.m.	Shopping in lunch hour
2–3 p.m.	Work
3–4 p.m.	Work
4–5 p.m.	Work
5–6 p.m.	Picked up dry cleaning
6–7 p.m.	Went to gym
7–8 p.m.	Cooking, eating & washing up
8–9 p.m.	TV
9–10 p.m.	TV
10–11 p.m.	Fell asleep on sofa
11–12 a.m.	Went to bed

Over the longer term you'll need to challenge your stress-related thoughts in much the same way as we've described for other negative thoughts. What is so bad about stress? What do you think it means? Do you see stress as a sign of weakness and inability to cope? Do you worry that it'll lead to a heart attack? What evidence do you have to support your beliefs? What might be evidence to the contrary? Is there a more balanced or alternative view? Here are some facts that might help with this exercise:

- Stress is part of life! Feeling under stress is common and not an illness.
- Stress can increase the chances of many illnesses occurring, but this is often because of the changes in behavior that stress provokes. For instance, people tend to smoke or drink more or eat 'comfort' foods that are high in fat or carbohydrates when they're stressed. There is also research to indicate that prolonged exposure to stress increases levels of cortisol (the stress hormone), which can affect and lower the immune system. That's why it's important to recognize and manage your stress as it occurs.
- Stress is not a sign of weakness. Stress affects everyone and anyone. A certain degree of stress is healthy and can in fact be helpful. It's what drives and motivates us to get things done. Some stress brings out the best in people and helps to give them the feeling that there are things in life worth striving for. But, like most things in life, it's good in moderation and bad in excess.

The next step is to identify your stress-related thoughts, challenge them and generate alternative viewpoints. Once you have done this you are part of the way towards managing your stress. The next stage is to develop further coping strategies. The two most obvious are time management (see page 167) and problem solving (see page 144).

Drugs and alcohol

Virtually all so-called recreational or illicit drugs have mind-altering properties. After all, that's why people take them. As such, they all have the potential to bring on DPAFU or make it worse. Cannabis (marijuana) may be used by some people because they find it relaxing. However, in our clinical experience cannabis above all other drugs, and especially the stronger forms (e.g. 'skunk') is most likely to cause DPAFU. Some people also find that it makes them anxious and paranoid.

The use of drugs and/or alcohol as a coping strategy may be very appealing for some people. In the short term they can appear useful in blotting out, or numbing, sensations associated with DPAFU. This is especially true when people feel they can't cope with these sensations. But drugs and alcohol are rarely, if ever, a helpful long-term strategy. On the other hand, many sufferers of DPAFU avoid drugs and/or alcohol altogether. Some people believe that taking illicit drugs, or drinking excessively, led to the onset of their DPAFU (see Jay's example on page 15). Others notice that even with one or two alcoholic drinks their symptoms or sensations of DPAFU increase. This can worry some people and lead to them avoiding alcohol at all costs. A few people in our clinic have remarked that it is the hangover stage that is particularly bad if you are prone to depersonalization. Abstaining from alcohol shouldn't be viewed as a problem in its own right, but it can become an issue. Think back to our discussion of safety-seeking behaviors. How does avoidance of alcohol fit with this? If you find yourself turning down invitations to social events because you no longer drink, ask yourself whether you're using it as an excuse not to go. If you think it may be an issue for you, try re-reading the section on avoidance and safety-seeking behaviors (page 33).

The usual approach when someone actively avoids a given situation because it increases anxiety is to encourage them to face it. In the case of illicit drug use this clearly wouldn't be appropriate. We don't advocate illicit activity, and neither do we advocate taking prescription medicine that has not been prescribed for you, nor taking too much of something that has been prescribed.

It's a bit different for alcohol. Drinking isn't a criminal activity and is often a big part of social life. But if used to excess it can be extremely harmful and can have far-reaching consequences. You'll need to exercise judgement in deciding what's right for you. If you find this difficult to do, you may wish to discuss the issue with friends, family or work colleagues. While specific advice on overcoming drink or drug problems is outside the scope of this book, we strongly advise you to seek professional help if you feel you're developing a problem with alcohol or drugs.

9

Other types of treatment

Psychological therapies

There are a wide variety of talking therapies and most of them are available on the NHS. They're usually delivered by either clinical psychologists, counselling psychologists, counsellors or nurses trained as therapists. However, if treatment is on the NHS, there'll be a waiting list and this may vary between two weeks to over a year. You will need to see your GP to get a referral to the local psychology, psychotherapy or counselling department. The therapy may take place at an outpatient unit within a local hospital, at your GP surgery or at a dedicated unit within the community. You may have a preference for the type of therapy you feel would best match your needs. Alternatively, you may have an assessment and the assessing team will advise on what they think would best suit you. The Department of Health produces a booklet entitled *Choosing Talking Therapies?* and it's well worth a read. You can access it from the Department of Health's website (see the section on Further Information on page 232).

Very briefly, one of the main therapies is *counselling*, which focuses on your problems in the here and now. You will be encouraged to talk about how you feel. The therapist will tend not to tell you what to do, such as suggesting coping strategies, but will instead allow you the space to explore how you feel and the impact this has on your life. Therapy lasts between 6–12 sessions and isn't especially intensive. Theoretically, counselling is a person-centred technique, but the counsellor may have a preference for either a more cognitive behavioral approach (and will use strategies similar to those we've described in this book) or psychodynamically orientated therapy, where the emphasis is on exploring early relationships and the effect they have on you now. Counsellors should have undertaken a recognized training course and be registered with an appropriate body (such as the British Association for Counselling and Psychotherapy), to whom they are accountable. This is particularly important if you decide to obtain private counselling because it's not illegal for anyone to call themselves a counsellor!

It is, however, illegal for someone to call themselves a *clinical psychologist* without the proper training. It takes three years of full-time training, in addition to an undergraduate degree in psychology, to become a clinical psychologist. Training includes a large research project that's equivalent to a PhD. The British Psychological Society holds a register of people allowed to practise as a clinical psychologist and it also regulates them. However, someone who has completed an undergraduate degree in the subject and has no clinical training may call themselves a psychologist. Again, this is something to be aware of if you look for a therapist privately. If you see a therapist via the NHS, their employers will have checked out their qualifications. By the way, a *psychiatrist* is a medically qualified specialist in mental health problems. Some psychiatrists have additional qualifications and experience in various therapies, but all will have a working knowledge of psychological treatments and the use of medication. In the UK the main qualification is membership of the Royal College of Psychiatrists (MRCPsych).

Other than CBT, the main therapy offered is either

psychodynamic or *psychoanalytic psychotherapy*. Psychotherapy usually involves exploring the connections between your present feelings and behaviors and past events and early relationships in your life. It aims to provide you with a greater understanding of yourself. Some therapists say very little and are more interpretive and analytical, focusing on the underlying meanings of what you say and do, while others are more interactive and supportive. This form of therapy may last from 16 weeks to several years and may be either one-to-one or in a group. It can be effective for people with long-term difficulties such as relationship problems, low self-esteem, and depression. Some people find this form of treatment difficult because you'll be expected to talk about potentially painful past experiences without necessarily being given the tools to help you cope. Instead you have to self-manage your emotions during the course of the therapy.

There are other forms of therapy that are well-respected but not always routinely available on the NHS, such as *cognitive analytic therapy* (CAT). This is a form of psychotherapy that blends the principles of CBT and psychoanalysis. It's analytical, but it also uses some of the tools and coping strategies of CBT. You may also come across systemic, humanistic, experiential or interpersonal psychotherapy, and art, drama or music therapy groups may also be available. These are all forms of psychotherapy that may be available to you either privately or on the NHS. Each has a distinct theoretical perspective that guides therapy. Because so little research has been conducted into the treatment of DPAFU we're not in a position to say if any or all of these forms of therapy would be of benefit and so we don't go into detail about them here. A useful book that describes the variety of talking therapies is *Individual Therapy: A Handbook*, edited by Windy Dryden.

There are risks associated with all talking therapies. You may well feel worse when you begin to talk about your problems. You may also begin to have difficulties in your relationships as you begin to change as a person. It is not uncommon to experience strong feelings of guilt, shame or anger during therapy, as these may have been previously kept under wraps. This may be particularly true with DPAFU because the main benefit of feeling numb is, of course, that you don't feel anything. If you begin to deal with all the feelings you have protected yourself from for so long, you may very well feel worse before feeling better. But beware of stopping the therapy before you've had a proper chance to see whether it can help you.

Medication

DPAFU involves a change in the state of mind. Because our brain activity provides the basis for our states of mind, experiencing DPAFU is associated with changes in the brain. This isn't to say that there is anything physically wrong with the brain. Indeed all the evidence suggests that the brain appears physically normal in people with DPAFU. However it seems likely that parts of the brain behave differently when people are experiencing the sensations of DPAFU compared to when they are not. This is probably because of the way different parts of the brain communicate with each other. Communication between parts of the brain involves chemicals called *neurotransmitters*. There are many different kinds of neurotransmitter, and medication works by changing the amount, or the activity, of one or more of them. In this way, medication can help treat a range of psychological problems, such as depression or anxiety.

Are there any medications that might be helpful for people with DPAFU?

The first thing to say is that there is currently no well-established drug treatment for DPAFU. At the time of writing, no medication has been specifically licensed (i.e. approved by the regulating authorities) to tackle DPAFU. *It is therefore essential that any drug treatment is undertaken with specialist supervision.* Having said this, there has been some research on possible treatments. A number of medications have been reported as being helpful in individual cases, but it is difficult to know whether these success stories can tell us much about DPAFU in general. For example, in one individual there is no way of knowing whether the person would have improved anyway, with or without the medication. To really know whether a medication is helpful, we need to look at larger studies. A few drugs have been studied for possible beneficial effects in treating DPAFU, including *fluoxetine* (Prozac) and *clomipramine* (Anafranil), but the results have not been particularly encouraging.

Clomipramine is an example of a tricycic antidepressant, as are *amitriptyline, nortriptyline, doxepin* and *imipramine*. *Fluoxetine* is an example of a serotonin re-uptake inhibitor (SSRI), as are *citalopram, sertraline* and *paroxetine*. There are other drugs called mono-amine oxidase inhibitors (MAOIs), such as *phenelzine*, and serotonin and noradrenaline re-uptake inhibitors (SNRIs), for example *venlafaxine*.

The main use of all of these classes of drug is to treat depression. Most have been around for many years and all have passed international standards of safety and efficacy. They all need to be prescribed by a qualified doctor. They all have side effects and certain benefits and drawbacks. For further information, see Appendix II.

Your doctor may have prescribed one or more of these drugs to you for depression, or a mixture of depression and anxiety or even to help with sleep problems or physical symptoms like chronic pain. If your doctor feels that one of these conditions underlies your DPAFU then that obviously makes sense. What we can say however is that, if you're only suffering from depersonalization, and if the depersonalization is relatively severe, these drugs don't always work.

One medication that has shown promising results in treating DPAFU is *lamotrigine* (Lamictal). Lamotrigine works primarily by influencing a neurotransmitter called glutamate.

Lamotrigine was originally designed to treat certain kinds of epilepsy, but its use in DPAFU doesn't mean that DPAFU is a form of epilepsy. The idea of using lamotrigine to treat DPAFU came from the discovery that it can prevent the depersonalization usually caused by ketamine (an anaesthetic drug that's sometimes used illicitly at clubs or raves). This led us to wonder whether lamotrigine might be helpful to people with DPAFU. Early observations were sufficiently encouraging for us to make lamotrigine a regular choice of drug treatment for DPAFU. We now have considerable experience in the use of lamotrigine for DPAFU and have conducted three studies of its effectiveness. Overall we've found that lamotrigine has a beneficial effect in around 50 per cent of people with DPAFU, but this figure rises to around 70 per cent when lamotrigine is combined with an antidepressant medication such as *citalopram*. These figures suggest that, although lamotrigine isn't a wonder drug, it can have a useful role in treating DPAFU, either by itself or in combination with another medication. However it should only be prescribed by a specialist, that is a psychiatrist who is able to supervise the treatment, make changes and monitor progress as appropriate. We repeat, *lamotrigine is not licensed for the treatment of DPAFU*.

When people first start taking lamotrigine, they should begin with a small dose of 25 mg per day. This is increased by 25 mg every two weeks, so that after two weeks they will start taking 50 mg per day, then two weeks after that the dose will rise to 75 mg per day, and so on. Once the dose is over 100 mg per day, further increases can safely be made in steps of 50 mg every two weeks. The maximum dose used in our clinic is around 400 mg per day. The reason for building the dose up gradually like this is that it reduces the risk of side effects. This is important because lamotrigine can cause a disorder of the blood cells – this happens to about 1 in 2,000 people who take it. To guard against this, the dose is built up slowly and people taking lamotrigine are advised to have blood tests in the early stages of treatment. The tests monitor their blood cell counts and their liver and kidney function. Another possible side effect of lamotrigine is a skin rash. Occasionally this may be serious, and for this reason anyone taking lamotrigine is advised to stop taking it immediately if a rash develops. Having said that, it should be stressed that the vast majority of people who take lamotrigine do so without experiencing unpleasant side effects.

In the early stages of treatment, most people feel little or no benefit from the lamotrigine. Usually it's not until the dose reaches 100 mg per day that people notice some reduction in their symptoms of DPAFU. The 'right dose' varies between individuals. Most people who benefit significantly from lamotrigine do so at a dose of between 200 and 400 mg per day, but others need a much higher dose. Some people report that the symptoms of DPAFU have completely lifted, while others say that the symptoms are still present, but are less intense and have less of an impact on their lives. When people have a good response to lamotrigine, we advise them to stay on the medication for a year before gradually reducing the dose down to zero. The withdrawal can be done over a period of two or three weeks.

As we've said, some people do not respond to lamotrigine, but at present we have no reliable way of predicting who will respond to it and who won't. However, if lamotrigine doesn't help, there are various other possible drugs. *Clonazepam* (Rivotril, Klonopin) is another epilepsy medication, although it works in a different way to lamotrigine. As well as its role in treating epilepsy, it's useful for controlling anxiety and agitation. We saw earlier in this book (see page 119) that there's often a relationship between anxiety and DPAFU. Clonazepam can be very effective in reducing anxiety, and some people with DPAFU find that it also decreases their DPAFU symptoms.

As with lamotrigine, there is a range of possible doses. Most people take between 1 mg and 8 mgs per day, either as a single dose or split between morning and evening doses. Clonazepam can be very helpful, but it's important to know that in some people it can become habit-forming and that coming off it may involve a period of gradual withdrawal by dose reduction. Use of clonazepam should be carefully discussed with your GP or psychiatrist before starting treatment. Once again, we must emphasize that *clonazepam is not licensed for the treatment of DPAFU.*

Another medication that may help with DPAFU is *naltrexone* (Nalorex). Two small studies have shown some evidence of a beneficial effect in DPAFU. However, at the time of writing information on its effectiveness in treating DPAFU is very limited. We are currently studying it as a possible treatment for DPAFU and hope to have more information available in the near future.

'Major tranquilliser' or 'antipsychotic' medications such as *chlorpromazine, olanzapine,* or *risperidone* are usually used to treat serious mental illnesses such as schizophrenia, and are not recommended for DPAFU. There is currently no theoretical reason for believing they will be helpful, and people with DPAFU who have been prescribed these drugs in the past have usually told us that they brought about a worsening of the symptoms. If you've been prescribed one of these drugs, it may be that your problems go beyond simple depersonalization or derealization. If you have any concerns, you should discuss them with your doctor. You should certainly not stop any part of your treatment before seeking such advice.

To sum up, various medications can be helpful for DPAFU. To date, the best results we've obtained in our specialist clinic have been with lamotrigine, particularly when it's given in combination with an antidepressant. If lamotrigine doesn't prove helpful, there are alternatives that can be tried. There is no reason why medication cannot be combined with psychological treatment, in fact it is probably best if it is combined in this way, although some people prefer to undertake one mode of treatment – psychological or pharmacological (drug-based) – without the other.

You should discuss your sensations of DPAFU with your doctor before taking any medication. Remember to tell him or her if you are taking any other medications, as some medications can interact with those discussed here. Also be sure to mention if you are pregnant or breastfeeding, because some medications should be avoided at these times.

Other physiological treatments

We've been studying some new treatment approaches in the Depersonalisation Disorder clinic at the Maudsley Hospital, one of which is *biofeedback*. This is based on the fact that people can learn to control certain bodily functions – such as pulse rate, blood pressure and reactions to emotions – if these measures are fed back to the person, and changes are displayed, in an easily accessible way. For example, if someone can actually hear their heartbeat, they may find that something they do (it doesn't matter what) makes it go up or down. The body then learns what it is that makes a difference, especially if this is rewarded in some way, through a kind of unconscious learning.

Biofeedback training has proved to be valuable in the treatment of a range of clinical conditions such as hypertension (high blood pressure), migraine headache, and even epilepsy. We described in Part 1 (see page 25) how our research has shown that DPAFU is characterized by reduced body arousal (arousal is the body gearing itself up for action) and reactions to emotions. We have started to investigate whether increasing body arousal may help relieve some of the symptoms of DPAFU. The person sits in front of a computer screen while electrodes from the skin of their hand convey to the computer skin conductance (arousal) levels. The person can then increase conductance levels and this is displayed in the form of a computer game. The sessions take between 20–40 minutes and have to be repeated several times to make a difference. Preliminary results suggest that it may be an effective treatment – at least in the short term. Clinical trials are currently underway.

Appendix I

The Cambridge Depersonalization Scale

CAMBRIDGE DEPERSONALIZATION SCALE
(State Version)

The wording of the scale has been amended slightly from the original to improve clarity

NAME: _____ AGE: _____
(please circle as required)   SEX: male / female

SCHOOLING: primary / secondary / higher
(e.g. university) (please circle as required)

PLEASE READ INSTRUCTIONS CAREFULLY:
This questionnaire describes strange and 'funny' feelings that people may have in their daily life. Please read carefully each of the following descriptions. If you feel you are having *right now* any of the following experiences, please let us know how bad it is at the moment by making a mark on the line.

Example:

0% _____/_____ 100%
(*I'm not having it at all*)   (*It's as bad as it can get*)

1 I'm feeling strange, as if I were not real or as if I were cut off from the world. Please mark the line to show the present intensity of this experience.

0% |_____| _____| 100%

2 Things around me are now looking 'flat' or 'lifeless', as if I were looking at a picture. Please mark the line to show the present intensity of this experience.

0% |_____| _____| 100%

3 I am feeling as if parts of my body don't belong to me. Please mark the line to show the present intensity of this experience.

0% |_____| _____| 100%

4 I'm now having the feeling of being a 'detached observer' of myself.

0% |_____| _____| 100%

5 My body is feeling very light now, as if I were floating on air.

0% |_____| _____| 100%

6 I am not feeling any emotions at all.

0% |_____| _____| 100%

7 If I read this sentence aloud, my voice sounds remote and unreal.

0% |_____| _____| 100%

8 I am having a feeling of complete emptiness in my head so that *I am not having any thoughts at all.*

0% | _____ | _____ | 100%

9 I'm having the feeling that my hands or my feet have become larger or smaller.

0% | _____ | _____ | 100%

10 My surroundings are feeling detached or unreal, as if there was a veil or a fog between me and the outside world.

0% | _____ | _____ | 100%

11 It seems now as if things that I have recently done took place a long time ago. For example anything which I have done this morning feels as if it were done weeks ago.

0% | _____ | _____ | 100%

12 If I now try to remember important events in my life (e.g. graduation, wedding etc.), I feel so detached from the memories that it seems as if I had not been involved in them.

0% | _____ | _____ | 100%

13 I don't seem to be feeling any affection towards my family and close friends.

0% | _____ | _____ | 100%

14 Objects around me are looking smaller or further away.

0% | _____ | _____ | 100%

15 I cannot feel properly the pencil that I have in my hand, as *if it were not me* who were holding it.

0% | _____ | _____ | 100%

16 If I now try to imagine the face of a relative or friend whom I frequently see (but who is not with me at present), I do not seem able to picture it in my mind.

0% | _____ | _____ | 100%

17 If I pinch myself in my arm now, I feel so detached from the pain that it feels as if it were 'somebody else's pain.'

0% | _____ | _____ | 100%

18 I am now having the feeling of being outside my body.

0% | _____ | _____ | 100%

19 I am feeling as if I were not in charge of my movements, so that I feel 'automatic' and mechanical, as if I were a 'robot'.

0% | _____ | _____ | 100%

20 I am feeling so detached from my thoughts that they seem to have a 'life' of their own.

0% | _____ | _____ | 100%

21 I feel like touching myself to make sure that I have a body or a real existence.

0% | _____ | _____ | 100%

22 I am still having the same strange feeling as when I started to answer this questionnaire.

0% | _____ | _____ | 100%

DEPERSONALIZATION SCALE (trait version)

The wording of the scale has been amended slightly from the original to improve clarity

NAME: _____ AGE: _____

(please circle as required)

SEX: male / female

SCHOOLING: primary / secondary / higher
(e.g. university) (please circle as required)

PLEASE READ INSTRUCTIONS CAREFULLY:

This questionnaire describes strange and 'funny' experiences that normal people may have in their daily life. We are interested in their (a) frequency, i.e. how often you have had these experiences *over the last six months;* and (b) their approximate duration. For each question, please circle the answers that suit you best. If you are not sure, give your best guess.

1 Out of the blue, I feel strange, as if I were not real or as if I were cut off from the world.

Frequency	Duration
0 = *never*	In general, it lasts:
1 = *rarely*	1 = *few seconds*
2 = *often*	2 = *few minutes*
3 = *very often*	3 = *few hours*
4 = *all the time*	4 = *about a day*
	5 = *more than a day*
	6 = *more than a week*

2 What I see looks 'flat' or 'lifeless', as if I were looking at a picture.

Frequency
0 = *never*
1 = *rarely*
2 = *often*
3 = *very often*
4 = *all the time*

Duration
In general, it lasts:
1 = *few seconds*
2 = *few minutes*
3 = *few hours*
4 = *about a day*
5 = *more than a day*
6 = *more than a week*

3 Parts of my body feel as if they don't belong to me.

Frequency
0 = *never*
1 = *rarely*
2 = *often*
3 = *very often*
4 = *all the time*

Duration
In general, it lasts:
1 = *few seconds*
2 = *few minutes*
3 = *few hours*
4 = *about a day*
5 = *more than a day*
6 = *more than a week*

4 I have found myself *not being frightened at all* in situations, which normally I would find frightening or distressing.

Frequency
0 = *never*
1 = *rarely*
2 = *often*
3 = *very often*
4 = *all the time*

Duration
In general, it lasts:
1 = *few seconds*
2 = *few minutes*
3 = *few hours*
4 = *about a day*
5 = *more than a day*
6 = *more than a week*

5 My favourite activities are no longer enjoyable.

Frequency
0 = *never*
1 = *rarely*
2 = *often*
3 = *very often*
4 = *all the time*

Duration
In general, it lasts:
1 = *few seconds*
2 = *few minutes*
3 = *few hours*
4 = *about a day*
5 = *more than a day*
6 = *more than a week*

6 While doing something I have the feeling of being a 'detached observer' of myself.

Frequency
0 = *never*
1 = *rarely*
2 = *often*
3 = *very often*
4 = *all the time*

Duration
In general, it lasts:
1 = *few seconds*
2 = *few minutes*
3 = *few hours*
4 = *about a day*
5 = *more than a day*
6 = *more than a week*

7 The flavour of meals no longer gives me a feeling of pleasure or distaste.

Frequency
0 = *never*
1 = *rarely*
2 = *often*
3 = *very often*
4 = *all the time*

Duration
In general, it lasts:
1 = *few seconds*
2 = *few minutes*
3 = *few hours*
4 = *about a day*
5 = *more than a day*
6 = *more than a week*

8 My body feels very light, as if it were floating on air.

Frequency
0 = *never*
1 = *rarely*
2 = *often*
3 = *very often*
4 = *all the time*

Duration
In general, it lasts:
1 = *few seconds*
2 = *few minutes*
3 = *few hours*
4 = *about a day*
5 = *more than a day*
6 = *more than a week*

9 When I weep or laugh, I do not seem *to feel* any emotions at all.

Frequency
0 = *never*
1 = *rarely*
2 = *often*
3 = *very often*
4 = *all the time*

Duration
In general, it lasts:
1 = *few seconds*
2 = *few minutes*
3 = *few hours*
4 = *about a day*
5 = *more than a day*
6 = *more than a week*

10 I have the feeling of *not having any thoughts at all*, so that when I speak it feels as if my words were being uttered by an 'automaton'.

Frequency
0 = *never*
1 = *rarely*
2 = *often*
3 = *very often*
4 = *all the time*

Duration
In general, it lasts:
1 = *few seconds*
2 = *few minutes*
3 = *few hours*
4 = *about a day*
5 = *more than a day*
6 = *more than a week*

11 Familiar voices (including my own) sound remote and unreal.

Frequency	Duration
0 = *never*	**In general, it lasts:**
1 = *rarely*	1 = *few seconds*
2 = *often*	2 = *few minutes*
3 = *very often*	3 = *few hours*
4 = *all the time*	4 = *about a day*
	5 = *more than a day*
	6 = *more than a week*

12 I have the feeling that my hands or my feet have become larger or smaller.

Frequency	Duration
0 = *never*	**In general, it lasts:**
1 = *rarely*	1 = *few seconds*
2 = *often*	2 = *few minutes*
3 = *very often*	3 = *few hours*
4 = *all the time*	4 = *about a day*
	5 = *more than a day*
	6 = *more than a week*

13 My surroundings feel detached or unreal, as if there was a veil between me and the outside world.

Frequency	Duration
0 = *never*	**In general, it lasts:**
1 = *rarely*	1 = *few seconds*
2 = *often*	2 = *few minutes*
3 = *very often*	3 = *few hours*
4 = *all the time*	4 = *about a day*
	5 = *more than a day*
	6 = *more than a week*

14 It seems as if things that I have recently done took place a long time ago. For example anything which I have done this morning feels as if it were done weeks ago.

Frequency	Duration
0 = *never*	**In general, it lasts:**
1 = *rarely*	1 = *few seconds*
2 = *often*	2 = *few minutes*
3 = *very often*	3 = *few hours*
4 = *all the time*	4 = *about a day*
	5 = *more than a day*
	6 = *more than a week*

15 While fully awake I have 'visions' in which I can see myself outside, as if I were looking at my image in a mirror.

Frequency	Duration
0 = *never*	**In general, it lasts:**
1 = *rarely*	1 = *few seconds*
2 = *often*	2 = *few minutes*
3 = *very often*	3 = *few hours*
4 = *all the time*	4 = *about a day*
	5 = *more than a day*
	6 = *more than a week*

16 I feel detached from memories of things that have happened to me – as if I had not been involved in them.

Frequency	Duration
0 = *never*	**In general, it lasts:**
1 = *rarely*	1 = *few seconds*
2 = *often*	2 = *few minutes*
3 = *very often*	3 = *few hours*
4 = *all the time*	4 = *about a day*
	5 = *more than a day*
	6 = *more than a week*

17 When in a new situation, it feels as if I have been through it before.

Frequency	Duration
0 = *never*	**In general, it lasts:**
1 = *rarely*	1 = *few seconds*
2 = *often*	2 = *few minutes*
3 = *very often*	3 = *few hours*
4 = *all the time*	4 = *about a day*
	5 = *more than a day*
	6 = *more than a week*

18 Out of the blue, I find myself not feeling any affection towards my family and close friends.

Frequency	Duration
0 = *never*	**In general, it lasts:**
1 = *rarely*	1 = *few seconds*
2 = *often*	2 = *few minutes*
3 = *very often*	3 = *few hours*
4 = *all the time*	4 = *about a day*
	5 = *more than a day*
	6 = *more than a week*

19 Objects around me seem to look smaller or further away.

Frequency	Duration
0 = *never*	**In general, it lasts:**
1 = *rarely*	1 = *few seconds*
2 = *often*	2 = *few minutes*
3 = *very often*	3 = *few hours*
4 = *all the time*	4 = *about a day*
	5 = *more than a day*
	6 = *more than a week*

20 I cannot feel properly the objects that I touch with my hands; it feels *as if it were not me* who is touching them.

Frequency	Duration
0 = *never*	**In general, it lasts:**
1 = *rarely*	1 = *few seconds*
2 = *often*	2 = *few minutes*
3 = *very often*	3 = *few hours*
4 = *all the time*	4 = *about a day*
	5 = *more than a day*
	6 = *more than a week*

21 I do not seem able to picture things in my mind, for example the face of a close friend or a familiar place.

Frequency	Duration
0 = *never*	**In general, it lasts:**
1 = *rarely*	1 = *few seconds*
2 = *often*	2 = *few minutes*
3 = *very often*	3 = *few hours*
4 = *all the time*	4 = *about a day*
	5 = *more than a day*
	6 = *more than a week*

22 When a part of my body hurts, I feel so detached from the pain that if feels as if it were somebody else's pain.

Frequency	Duration
0 = *never*	**In general, it lasts:**
1 = *rarely*	1 = *few seconds*
2 = *often*	2 = *few minutes*
3 = *very often*	3 = *few hours*
4 = *all the time*	4 = *about a day*
	5 = *more than a day*
	6 = *more than a week*

23 I have the feeling of being outside my body.

Frequency	Duration
0 = *never*	**In general, it lasts:**
1 = *rarely*	1 = *few seconds*
2 = *often*	2 = *few minutes*
3 = *very often*	3 = *few hours*
4 = *all the time*	4 = *about a day*
	5 = *more than a day*
	6 = *more than a week*

24 When I move it doesn't feel as if I am in charge of the movements, so that I feel 'automatic' and mechanical, as if I were a robot.

Frequency	Duration
0 = *never*	**In general, it lasts:**
1 = *rarely*	1 = *few seconds*
2 = *often*	2 = *few minutes*
3 = *very often*	3 = *few hours*
4 = *all the time*	4 = *about a day*
	5 = *more than a day*
	6 = *more than a week*

25 The smell of things no longer gives me a feeling of pleasure or dislike.

Frequency	Duration
0 = *never*	**In general, it lasts:**
1 = *rarely*	1 = *few seconds*
2 = *often*	2 = *few minutes*
3 = *very often*	3 = *few hours*
4 = *all the time*	4 = *about a day*
	5 = *more than a day*
	6 = *more than a week*

26 I feel so detached from my thoughts that they seem to have a life of their own.

Frequency	Duration
0 = *never*	**In general, it lasts:**
1 = *rarely*	1 = *few seconds*
2 = *often*	2 = *few minutes*
3 = *very often*	3 = *few hours*
4 = *all the time*	4 = *about a day*
	5 = *more than a day*
	6 = *more than a week*

27 I have to touch myself to make sure that I have a body or a real existence.

Frequency	Duration
0 = *never*	**In general, it lasts:**
1 = *rarely*	1 = *few seconds*
2 = *often*	2 = *few minutes*
3 = *very often*	3 = *few hours*
4 = *all the time*	4 = *about a day*
	5 = *more than a day*
	6 = *more than a week*

28 I seem to have lost some bodily sensations (e.g. hunger and thirst), so that when I eat or drink it feels like an automatic routine.

Frequency	Duration
0 = *never*	**In general, it lasts:**
1 = *rarely*	1 = *few seconds*
2 = *often*	2 = *few minutes*
3 = *very often*	3 = *few hours*
4 = *all the time*	4 = *about a day*
	5 = *more than a day*
	6 = *more than a week*

29 Previously familiar places look unfamiliar, as if I had never seen them before.

Frequency	Duration
0 = *never*	**In general, it lasts:**
1 = *rarely*	1 = *few seconds*
2 = *often*	2 = *few minutes*
3 = *very often*	3 = *few hours*
4 = *all the time*	4 = *about a day*
	5 = *more than a day*
	6 = *more than a week*

Source: M. Sierra-Sieger and G. E. Berrios, 'The Cambridge Depersonalization Scale: a new instrument for the measurement of depersonalization', *Psychiatry Research*, 93 (2), pp. 153–64. Copyright Elsevier, 6 March 2000.

Appendix II

What are antidepressants?

This appendix is reproduced from the Royal College of Psychiatrists website:

www.rcpsych.ac.uk/mentalhealthinformation/mentalhealthproblems/depression/antidepressants.aspx

WHAT ARE ANTIDEPRESSANTS?

Antidepressants are drugs that relieve the symptoms of depression. They were first developed in the 1950s and have been used regularly since then. There are almost 30 different kinds of antidepressants available today and there are four main types:

- Tricycics
- MAOIs (Monoamine oxidase inhibitors)
- SSRIs (Selective serotonin re-uptake inhibitors)
- SNRIs (Serotonin and noradrenaline re-uptake inhibitors)

HOW DO THEY WORK?

We don't know for certain, but we think that antidepressants work by increasing the activity of certain chemicals in our brains called neurotransmitters. They pass signals from one brain cell to another. The chemicals most involved in depression are thought to be Serotonin and Noradreline.

WHAT ARE ANTIDEPRESSANTS USED FOR?

- Moderate to severe depressive illness (not mild depression).
- Severe anxiety and panic attacks.
- Obsessive compulsive disorders.
- Chronic pain.
- Eating disorders.
- Post-traumatic stress disorder.

If you are not clear about why an antidepressant has been suggested for you, ask your doctor.

HOW WELL DO THEY WORK?

After three months of treatment, the proportions of people with depression who will be much improved are:

- 50 per cent and 65 per cent if given an antidepressant *compared with*;
- 25–30 per cent if given an inactive 'dummy' pill, or placebo.

It may seem surprising that people given placebo tablets improve, but this happens with all tablets that affect how we feel – the effect is similar with painkillers. Antidepressants are helpful but, like many other medicines, some of the benefit is due to the placebo effect.

ARE THE NEWER ONES BETTER THAN THE OLDER ONES?

Yes and no. The older tablets (Tricycics) are just as effective as the newer ones (SSRIs) but, on the whole, the newer ones seem to have fewer side effects. A major advantage for the newer tablets is that they are not so dangerous if someone takes an overdose.

DO ANTIDEPRESSANTS HAVE SIDE EFFECTS?

Yes – your doctor will be able to advise you here. You should always remind him or her of any medical conditions you have or have had in the past. Listed below are the side effects you might experience with the different types of antidepressant.

Tricyclics

These commonly cause a dry mouth, a slight tremor, fast heartbeat, constipation, sleepiness, and weight gain. Particularly in older people, they may cause confusion, slowness in starting and stopping when passing water, faintness through low blood pressure, and falls. If you have heart trouble, it may be best not to take one of this group of antidepressants. Men may experience difficulty in getting or keeping an erection, or delayed ejaculation. Tricycic antidepressants are dangerous in overdose.

SSRIs

During the first couple of weeks of taking them, you may feel sick and more anxious. Some of these tablets can produce nasty indigestion, but you can usually stop this by taking them with food. More seriously, they may interfere with your sexual function. There have been reports of episodes of aggression, although these are rare.

The list of side effects looks worrying – there is even more information about these on the leaflets that come with the medication. However, most people get a small number of mild side effects (if any). The side effects usually wear off over a couple of weeks as your body gets used to the medication. It is important to have this whole list, though, so you can recognize side effects if they happen. You can then talk them over with your doctor. The more serious ones – problems with urinating, difficulty in remembering, falls, confusion – are uncommon in healthy, younger or middle-aged people. It is common, if you are depressed, to think of harming or killing yourself. Tell your doctor – suicidal thoughts will pass once the depression starts to lift.

SNRIs

The side effects are very similar to the SSRIs, but Venlafaxine is not recommended for people who have heart problems, high blood pressure or problems with the salt levels in their blood. They can be helpful if other antidepressants have failed but they should only be prescribed by doctors with special experience in mental health.

MAOIs

This type of antidepressant is rarely prescribed these days. MAOIs can give you a dangerously high blood pressure if you eat foods containing a substance called Tyramine. If you agree to take an MAOI antidepressant your doctor will give you a list of foods to avoid.

WHAT ABOUT DRIVING OR OPERATING MACHINERY?

Some antidepressants make you sleepy and slow down your reactions – the older ones are more likely to do this. Some can be taken if you are driving. Remember, depression itself will interfere with your concentration and make it more likely that you will have an accident. If in doubt, check with your doctor.

ARE ANTIDEPRESSANTS ADDICTIVE?

Antidepressant drugs don't cause the addictions that you get with tranquillisers, alcohol or nicotine, in the sense that:

- You don't need to keep increasing the dose to get the same effect.
- You won't find yourself craving them if you stop taking them.

However, there is a debate about this. In spite of not having the symptoms of addiction described above, up to a third of people who stop SSRIs and SNRIs have withdrawal symptoms.

These include:

- Stomach upsets.
- Flu like symptoms.
- Anxiety.
- Dizziness.
- Vivid dreams at night.
- Sensations in the body that feel like electric shocks.

In most people these withdrawal effects are mild, but for a small number of people they can be quite severe. They seem to be most likely to happen with Paroxetine (Seroxat) and

Venlafaxine (Efexor). It is generally best to taper off the dose of an antidepressant rather than stop it suddenly.

Some people have reported that, after taking an SSRI for several months, they have had difficulty managing once the drug has been stopped and so feel they are addicted to it. Most doctors would say that it is more likely that the original condition has returned.

The Committee of Safety of Medicines in the UK reviewed the evidence in 2004 and concluded: 'There is no clear evidence that the SSRIs and related antidepressants have a significant dependence liability or show development of a dependence syndrome according to internationally accepted criteria.'

SSRI ANTIDEPRESSANTS, SUICIDAL FEELINGS AND YOUNG PEOPLE

There is some evidence of increased suicidal thoughts (although not actual suicidal acts) and other side effects in young people taking antidepressants. So, SSRI antidepressants are not licensed for use in people under 18. However, the National Institute for Clinical Excellence has stated that Fluoxetine, an SSRI antidepressant, can be used in the under-18s.

There is no clear evidence of an increased risk of self-harm and suicidal thoughts in adults of 18 years or over. But individuals mature at different rates. Young adults are more likely to commit suicide than older adults, so a young adult should be particularly closely monitored if he or she takes an SSRI antidepressant.

WHAT ABOUT PREGNANCY?

It is always best to take as little as possible in the way of medication during pregnancy, especially during the first three months. There is recent evidence of an increase in congenital malformations in babies of mothers who took antidepressants during this time. However, some mothers do have to take antidepressants during pregnancy and the risks need to be balanced. There is also some evidence that babies of mothers taking antidepressants may experience withdrawal symptoms soon after birth. Just as adults, this seems to be more likely if Paroxetine is the antidepressant being taken. Until we know more, doctors have been advised to consider alternative treatment in pregnancy.

WHAT ABOUT BREASTFEEDING?

Women commonly become depressed after giving birth – this is called post-natal depression. It usually gets better with counselling and practical support.

However, if you are unlucky enough to get it badly, it can exhaust you, stop you from breastfeeding, upset your relationship with your baby and even hold back your baby's development. In this case, antidepressants can be helpful.

WHAT ABOUT THE BABY?

He or she will get only a small amount of antidepressant from mother's milk. Babies older than a few weeks have very effective kidneys and livers. They are able to break down and get rid of medicines just as adults do, so the risk to the baby is very small. Some antidepressants are better than others in this regard and it is worth discussing this with your doctor or pharmacist. On balance, bearing in mind all the advantages of breastfeeding, it seems best to carry on with it while taking antidepressants.

HOW SHOULD ANTIDEPRESSANTS BE TAKEN?

- Keep in touch with your doctor in the first few weeks. With some of the older Tricycic drugs it's best to start on a lower dose and work upwards over the next couple of weeks. If you don't go back to the doctor and have the dose increased, you could end up taking too little. You usually don't have to do this with the SSRI tablets. The dose you start with is usually the dose you carry on with. It doesn't help to increase the dose above the recommended levels.
- Try not to be put off if you get some side effects. Many of them wear off in a few days. Don't stop the tablets unless the side effects really are unpleasant. If they are, get an urgent appointment to see your doctor. If you feel worse it is important to tell your doctor so that he or she can decide if the medicines are right for you. Your doctor will also want to know if you get increased feelings of restlessness or agitation.
- Take them every day – if you don't, they won't work.
- Wait for them to work. They don't work straight away. Most people find that they take one to two weeks to start working and maybe up to six weeks to give their full effect.
- Persevere – stopping too early is the commonest reason for people not getting better and for the depression to return.
- Try not to drink alcohol. Alcohol on its own can make your depression worse, but it can also make you slow and drowsy if you are taking antidepressants. This can lead to problems with driving – or with anything you need to concentrate on.
- Keep them out of the reach of children.

- Tempted to take an overdose? Tell your doctor as soon as possible and give your tablets to someone else to keep for you.
- Tell your doctor about any major changes in how you feel when the dose of antidepressant is changed.

HOW LONG WILL I HAVE TO TAKE THEM FOR?

Antidepressants don't necessarily treat the cause of the depression or take it away completely. Without any treatment, most depressions will get better after about eight months.

If you stop the medication before eight or nine months is up, the symptoms of depression are more likely to come back. The current recommendation is that it is best to take antidepressants for at least six months after you start to feel better. It is worthwhile thinking about what might have made you vulnerable, or might have helped to trigger off your depression. There may be ways of making this less likely to happen again.

If you have had two or more attacks of depression then treatment should be continued for at least two years.

WHAT IF THE DEPRESSION COMES BACK?

Some people have severe depressions over and over again. Even when they have got better, they may need to take antidepressants for several years to stop their depression coming back. This is particularly important in older people, who are more likely to have several periods of depression. For some people, other drugs such as Lithium may be recommended. Psychotherapy may be helpful in addition to the tablets.

SO WHAT IMPACT WOULD THESE TABLETS HAVE ON MY LIFE?

Depression is unpleasant. It can seriously affect your ability to work and enjoy life. Antidepressants can help you get better quicker. They can be prescribed by your GP and, apart from the side effects mentioned above, should have very little impact on your life. People on these tablets, particularly the newer ones, should be able to socialize, carry on at work, and enjoy their normal leisure activities.

If you have been depressed for a long time, others who know you well (for example your partner) may have got used to you being like this. Some people in this situation have reported that, as they got better and developed a more positive outlook, their partners had difficulty in adjusting to the change. This can cause friction and is something that people need to be aware of and discuss openly if it happens.

WHAT WILL HAPPEN IF I DON'T TAKE THEM?

It's difficult to say – so much depends on why they have been prescribed, on how bad your depression is and how long you've had it for. It's generally accepted that most depressions resolve themselves naturally within about eight months. If your depression is mild it is best to try some of the other treatments mentioned below. If you can't decide, talk it over with your doctor.

WHAT OTHER TREATMENTS OF DEPRESSION ARE AVAILABLE?

It is not enough just to take the pills. It is important to find ways of making yourself feel better, so you are less likely to become depressed again. These can include finding someone you can talk to, taking regular exercise, drinking less alcohol, eating well, using self-help techniques to help you relax and finding ways to solve the problems that have brought the depression on.

Appendix III

Blank worksheets

On the following pages you'll find a series of blank worksheets for the exercises described in Part 2.

TABLE 6.2: MEASURING THE INTENSITY OF DPAFU	
Numerical value	PROBLEMATIC SENSATION
0	
1	
2	
3	
4	
5	
6	
7	
8	
9	
10	

TABLE 6.4: RECORDING SPECIFIC SENSATIONS AND BEHAVIORS

Sensation	Makes you do more	Makes you do less	

TABLE 6.6: GOAL-SETTING SHEET

Problematic sensation Current score 0–10 Target score 0–10	Increased activities	Decreased activities

TABLE 6.8: HOURLY DPAFU DIARY

Rate your DPAFU every hour using the scale below:

0 —— 1 —— 2 —— 3 —— 4 —— 5 —— 6 —— 7 —— 8 —— 9 —— 10
No DPAFU at all   Moderate DPAFU   Worst DPAFU

Time	Monday	Tuesday	Wednesday	Thursday	Friday	Saturday	Sunday
6–7 a.m.							
7–8 a.m.							
8–9 a.m.							
9–10 a.m.							
10–11 a.m.							
11–12 p.m.							
12–1 p.m.							
1–2 p.m.							

2–3 p.m.	3–4 p.m.	4–5 p.m.	5–6 p.m.	6–7 p.m.	7–8 p.m.	8–9 p.m.	9–10 p.m.	10–11 p.m.	11–12 a.m.	12–1 a.m.

TABLE 6.10: STEBS DIARY

Situation	Thoughts	Emotion	Behaviors	Sensations

TABLE 6.13: CHALLENGING AUTOMATIC THOUGHTS

Negative automatic thought (NAT)	Moods	Evidence for	Evidence against	Balanced thought	Strength of original NAT

TABLE 6.15: THOUGHT RECORD

1. Situation (when/where/what/with whom)	2. Moods strength (0–100%)	3. Negative automatic thought (NAT) and strength of belief (0–100%)	4. Evidence for the NAT	5. Evidence against the NAT	6. Alternative or balanced thought and strength of belief (0–100%)	7. Strength of old NAT (0–100%)

TABLE 6.17: BEHAVIORAL EXPERIMENT WORKSHEET					
Target behavior	Assumption being tested	Belief in assumption (%)	Experiment	Outcome of experiment	New belief in assumption (%)

TABLE 6.19: DAY FROM A WEEKLY ACTIVITY DIARY

Day and Date:

Time	Activity	Mood	Pleasure	Achievement
6–7 a.m.				
7–8 a.m.				
8–9 a.m.				
9–10 a.m.				
10–11 a.m.				
11–12 p.m.				
12–1 p.m.				
1–2 p.m.				
2–3 p.m.				
3–4 p.m.				
4–5 p.m.				
5–6 p.m.				
6–7 p.m.				
7–8 p.m.				
8–9 p.m.				
9–10 p.m.				
10–11 p.m.				
11–12 a.m.				

TABLE 8.3: STRESS DIARY

Day	Rating	Factors causing or maintaining stress
Mon		
Tue		
Wed		
Thurs		
Fri		
Sat		
Sun		

Glossary

anxiety: a mood state, which can be brief or prolonged and characterized by negative feelings such as apprehension, dread, uneasiness and distress. Anxiety is related to fear, but unlike fear, a specific object, person or event does not always induce it.

attribution: a statement or belief that something causes something else to happen, or explains it.

avoidance: the tendency not to do something, or keep away from something that we believe is likely to result in a negative outcome. For example, we may not take an exam because we believe that the most likely outcome is failure, or we may avoid leaving the house because we fear that we would not be able to cope.

cognitive errors/distortions: these are common errors of thinking (or imagining) that happen automatically (*see* **NATs**). Examples of cognitive errors/distortions are 'jumping to conclusions' or 'believing that we know what others are thinking'. Although everyone makes these types of errors, they become more frequent and distorted when we experience negative emotional states.

delusion: a false belief that is maintained to the contrary of the available information and data, and despite what almost everyone with the same background argues. An example of a delusion would be the belief that intelligence forces are spying on you from outer space, or that you have supernatural powers.

depersonalization: the feeling of loss of the self or any aspect of the self and/or of one's identity.

depressive illness/depression: a state characterized by low mood which persists and is of such a severity that it interferes with day-to-day life. It is likely to be deemed to merit medical or psychological treatment.

derealization: an alteration in the perception of the environment and/or disconnection from it, such that it feels changed, altered or unreal.

dissociation/dissociative experiences: experiences that cover a range of sensations of feeling disconnected from oneself, others or the world. These can include the feeling of being outside, or separated from, your own body, personality, or functions, or forgetting who you are or what you have been doing over a period of time.

emotional reasoning: the belief that something is 'true' or 'real' because it feels emotionally as if that were the case. For example, believing that you are a complete failure just because you feel a sense of failure at the present moment.

hallucination: an experience of false perception which occurs when a person is wide awake. The experience is believed to be real but lacks the physical stimulus. Some common examples are hearing voices that are not present (*auditory hallucination*) or likewise seeing objects that are not present (*visual hallucination*). Any of the senses may be involved, including smell, taste, or touch.

low mood: a relatively short-lived mood state characterized by negative feelings such as sadness, depression, despondency, pessimism, self-doubt and/or hopelessness.

negative automatic thoughts (NATs): thoughts by their very nature are automatic in that they 'pop' into our head without control or volition. Negative automatic thoughts are distressing and tend to be linked to negative beliefs about ourselves, the world and/or others. These types of thought are likely to be biased in nature (*see* **cognitive errors/distortions**).

neurological: relating to the structure and function of the nervous system which encompasses the brain, spinal cord and peripheral nerves.

obsessive compulsive disorder (OCD): is a clinical condition. Obsessions are annoying thoughts or images that repeatedly enter the mind. Compulsions are useless behaviors – actions that you feel you have to do but find difficult to resist. They therefore tend to be repeated again and again.

phobia: a state of anxiety induced by a specific situation, object, or event.

psychosis: a generic term, often used by psychiatrists and psychologists to describe a range of conditions that are characterized by a combination of delusions, hallucinations, disorganized speech, unpredictable and/or disturbed behavior and mood. Examples of these conditions are schizophrenia and bipolar disorder.

recurrent DPAFU (depersonalization and/or feelings of unreality): feelings of depersonalization and/or derealization that continue to re-occur. Each episode may last for a substantial period of time.

rumination: dwelling upon thoughts, ideas, beliefs and/or images. This process is usually unwanted and/or intrusive and cannot be controlled or stopped at will.

safety-seeking behavior: any behavior that we adopt because we believe it is likely to prevent harm and/or something bad happening. Safety-seeking behaviors can be 'overt' and clearly observable by others, or 'covert' which means they only involve our thoughts. An example of an overt safety-seeking behavior might be taking sips of water because we believe it will prevent fainting. A covert safety-seeking behavior might be repeating specific words or counting to try to prevent something bad from happening. It is important to recognize that the safety-seeking behaviors themselves do not prevent harm from happening despite the belief that they do.

social anxiety/phobia: feelings of anxiety when placed in a 'social' or 'public' situation fed by the belief that one is likely to be judged negatively by others. A common example of this is a fear of embarrassing yourself while making a speech or giving a presentation.

transient DPAFU (depersonalization and/or feelings of unreality): feelings of depersonalization and/or derealization that come and go, and only last a very brief time.

Further information

Books

Cognitive Therapy of Anxiety Disorders: A Practice Manual and Conceptual Guide by A. Wells, Wiley (1997)

Feeling Unreal: Depersonalization Disorder and the Loss of the Self by D. Simeon and J. Abugel, Oxford University Press (2006)

Full Catastrophe Living by J. Kabat-Zinn, Piatkus (1996)

Handbook of Individual Therapy 4th Edition by W. Dryden, Sage Publications (2002)

Mind over Mood: Change How You Feel By Changing The Way You Think by D.A. Greenberger and C.A. Padesky, Guildford Press (1995)

10 Days to Great Self-Esteem by D. Burns, Vermillion (2000)

Other relevant books in the *Overcoming* series

Overcoming Anxiety by H. Kennerley, Constable & Robinson (2009)

Overcoming Childhood Trauma by H. Kennerley, Constable & Robinson (2000)

Overcoming Depression by P. Gilbert, Constable & Robinson (2009)

Overcoming Insomnia and Sleep Problems by C. Espie, Constable & Robinson (2006)

Overcoming Low Self-Esteem by M. Fennell, Constable & Robinson (2009)

Overcoming Traumatic Stress by C. Herbert and A. Wetmore, Constable & Robinson (1999)

Academic articles

Although many of these articles are intended for academics and scientists, they may be of interest to some people with DPAFU. In addition, if you are seeing a healthcare professional they may wish to track down some of the articles for themselves.

'Emotional memory in depersonalization disorder: a functional MRI study' by N. Medford, B. Brierley, M. Brammer, E. T. Bullmore, A. S. David and M. L. Phillips in *Psychiatry Research: Neuroimaging*, 2006, Volume 148, pp. 93–102.

This study explored our memory for emotional words and found that people who report DPAFU showed different brain activity to people who didn't when asked to remember previously read emotional words, or words within emotionally charged sentences.

'Lamotrigine as an add-on treatment for depersonalization disorder: a retrospective study of 32 cases' by M. Sierra, D. Baker, N. Medford, E. Lawrence, M. Patel, M. L. Phillips and A. S. David in *Clinical Neuropharmacology*, 2006, Volume 29, issue 5, pp. 253–8.

The results of this small trial suggest that a significant number of patients with DPAFU may respond to lamotrigine when combined with antidepressant medication. The results are sufficiently positive to prompt a larger controlled evaluation of lamotrigine as an 'add-on' treatment in DPAFU.

'Autonomic response in the perception of disgust and happiness in depersonalization disorder' by M. Sierra, C. Senior, M. L. Phillips and A. S. David in *Psychiatry Research*, 2006, Volume 145, pp. 225–31.

This study measured skin conductance (a measure of how the body reacts to emotions) in response to faces expressing happiness and disgust and found that people with DPAFU showed lowered responses to disgusted faces only. This is indicative of emotional numbing to unpleasant and threatening stimuli.

'Cognitive Behaviour Therapy for Depersonalisation Disorder: An Open Study' by E. Hunter, D. Baker, M. Phillips, M. Sierra and A. S.

David in *Behaviour Research and Therapy*, 2005, Volume 43, issue 9, pp. 1121–30.

This small-scale study explored the use of CBT for symptoms of DPAFU. The initial results suggest that a CBT approach to DPAFU may be effective, but further trials with larger sample sizes and more rigorous research methodology are needed to determine how useful it is.

'Understanding and treating depersonalisation disorder' by N. Medford, M. Sierra, D. Baker and A. S. David in *Advances in Psychiatric Treatment*, 2005, Volume 11, pp. 92–100.

A review paper introducing DPAFU and discussing various treatment options.

'Depersonalisation Disorder' by M. L. Phillips, E. Hunter, D. Baker, N. Medford, M. Sierra and A. S. David in *Current Medical Literature – Psychiatry*, 2005, Volume 16, issue 1, pp. 1–5.

A brief overview of the clinical features and prevalence of DPAFU, along with a review of the latest in drug and CBT treatments.

'Neuroplasticity: Changes in grey matter induced by training' by B. Draganski, C. Gaser, V. Busch, G. Schuierer, U. Bogdahn and A. May in *Nature*, 2004, Volume 427, pp. 311–12.

As we described on page 26, this brain imaging study of 12 healthy volunteers showed that the structure of the brain can change as a result of a person's behavior, in this case learning to juggle.

'The epidemiology of depersonalization and derealization: a systematic review' by E. Hunter, M. Sierra and A.S. David in *Social Psychiatry & Psychiatric Epidemiology*, 2004, Volume 39, issue 1, pp. 9–18.

Surveys demonstrate that short-lasting symptoms of DPAFU in the general population are common. In addition, DPAFU appears to be common in normal and psychiatric populations.

'Depersonalization Disorder: A Contemporary Overview' by D. Simeon in *CNS Drugs*, 2004, Volume 18, issue 6, pp. 343–54.

A review paper explaining the clinical manifestations, prevalence and potential treatment options.

'Fluoxetine therapy in depersonalisation disorder: Randomized controlled trial' by D. Simeon, O. Guralnik, J. Schmeidler and M.

Knutelska in *British Journal of Psychiatry*, 2004, Volume 185, issue 1, pp. 31–6.

Fifty-four participants were randomly given either fluoxetine or a placebo in a double blind trial (during the trial neither patients nor researchers knew who was taking real medication and who was taking a placebo). Fluoxetine was not effective in treating DPAFU.

'Depersonalisation Disorder: clinical features of 204 cases' by D. Baker, E. Hunter, E. J. Lawrence, N. Medford, M. Patel, C. Senior, M. Sierra, M. V. Lambert, M. L. Phillips and A. S. David in *British Journal of Psychiatry*, 2003, Volume 182, pp. 428–33.

This paper presents an overview of the clinical features of DPAFU drawn from responses to a questionnaire given to patients referred to our Unit at the Maudsley Hospital.

'Depersonalisation Disorder: A Cognitive–Behavioural Conceptualisation' by E. Hunter, M. Phillips, T. Chalder, M. Sierra and A. S. David in *Behavioural Research & Therapy*, 2003, Volume 41, issue 12, pp. 1451–67.

This paper presents a cognitive behavioral model of DPAFU.

'Chronic Depersonalization following illicit drug use: Review of Forty Cases' by N. Medford, D. Baker, E. Hunter, M. Sierra, E. J. Lawrence, M. L. Phillips and A. S. David in *Addiction*, 2003, Volume 98, issue 12, pp. 1731–36.

This study suggests that the nature of drug-induced DPAFU is not on the whole different from DPAFU that is not drug-induced.

'Feeling unreal: a depersonalisation disorder update of 117 cases' by D. Simeon, M. Knutelska, D. Nelson and O. Guralnik in *Journal of Clinical Psychiatry*, 2003, Volume 64, issue 9, pp. 990–7.

A report on the clinical characteristics and prevalence of DPAFU.

'Autonomic response in depersonalisation disorder' by M. Sierra, C. Senior, J. Dalton, M. McDonough, A. Bond, M. L. Phillips, A. M. O'Dwyer and A. S. David in *Archives of General Psychiatry*, 2002, Volume 59, issue 9, pp. 833–8.

This study measured skin conductance (a measure of emotional activation in the body) in response to disturbing pictures and found that people with DPAFU showed reduced responses indicative of 'emotional numbing'.

'Depersonalisation Disorder: Thinking without Feeling' by M. L. Phillips, N. Medford, C. Senior, E. T. Bullmore, J. Suckling, M. J. Brammer, C. Andrew, M. Sierra, S. C. R. Williams and A. S. David in *Psychiatry Research: Neuroimaging*, 2001, Volume 108, pp. 145–160.

One of the earliest fMRI (a type of brain scan that shows which areas are activated) studies of DPAFU, which showed underactivity in key emotion-processing brain regions.

'Depersonalisation research at the Maudsley Hospital' by C. Senior, E. Hunter, M. V. Lambert, N. C. Medford, M. Sierra, M. L. Phillips and A. S. David in *The Psychologist*, 2001, Volume 14, issue 3, pp. 128–32.

A non-specialist article reviewing the work of our Unit at the Maudsley Hospital.

'The Cambridge Depersonalization Scale. A new instrument for the measurement of depersonalisation' by M. Sierra-Siegert and G. Berrios in *Psychiatry Research*, 2000, Volume 93, pp. 153–64.

Introducing the Cambridge Depersonalization Scale – a self-report measure of DPAFU (see Appendix I).

'Development, reliability, and validity of a dissociation scale' by E. M. Bernstein and F. W. Putnam in *Journal of Nervous & Mental Disease*, 1986, Volume 174, pp. 727–35.

Describes and presents the Dissociative Experiences Scale (see page 12).

Classic historical books and articles

'Depersonalization: a conceptual history' by M. Sierra and G. E. Berrios in *History of Psychiatry*, 1997, Volume 8, pp. 213–29.

Reviews classic and modern writings.

'Depersonalization – I. aetiology and phenomenology; II. clinical syndromes' by B. Ackner in *Journal of Mental Science*, 1954, Volume 100, issue 1, pp. 838–53, (II) pp. 854–72.

Medical Psychology by P. Schilder, John Wiley & Sons (1953).

'On depersonalization' by W. W. Mayer-Gross in *British Journal of Medical Psychology*, 1935, Volume 15, pp. 103–22.

'The depersonalization syndrome' by H. J. Shorvon in *Proceedings of the Royal Society of Medicine*, 1946, Volume 39, pp. 779–92.

'Un cas de depersonnaliszation (by L Dugas)' by M. Sierra and G. Berrios in *History of Psychiatry* (Introduction and translation), 1996, Volume 7, pp. 451–61.
Reviews classic and modern writings.

Websites

Websites on depersonalization

Depersonalization Community (a DPAFU discussion site):
www.dpselfhelp.com/

DPAFU discussion site:
www.depersonalization.info/main.html

DPAFU Research Unit at the Maudsley Hospital:
www.iop.kcl.ac.uk/departments/?locator=911

Other Websites

beyond blue (a non-profit organization in Australia devoted to increasing awareness of depression):
www.beyondblue.org.au

The Centre for Mindfulness Research and Practice (CMRP):
www.bangor.ac.uk/mindfulness/

Department of Health (DoH): www.dh.gov.uk

DoH: *Choosing Talking Therapies* booklet: www.dh.gov.uk/en/Publicationsandstatistics/Publications/PublicationsPolicyAndGuidance/DH_4008162

everybody (provides consumer health information for New Zealanders):
www.everybody.co.nz

Mind (a mental health charity):
www.mind.org.uk

National Institute for Health and Clinical Excellence:
www.nice.org.uk

Pub-Med (free access to some scientific articles):
www.ncbi.nlm.nih.gov/entrez/query.fcgi

Rethink (a mental health charity):
www.rethink.org

The Royal College of Psychiatrists (RCP):
www.rcpsych.ac.uk

RCP antidepressants information:
www.rcpsych.ac.uk/mentalhealthinformation/mentalhealth
problems/depression/antidepressants.aspx

Organizations

UK

British Association for Behavioural and Cognitive Psychotherapies
(BABCP)
Imperial House
Hornby Street
Bury BL9 5BN
Tel.: 0161 705 4304
Email: babcp@babcp.com
Website: www.babcp.com

The British Psychological Society
St Andrews House
48 Princess Road East
Leicester LE1 7DR
Tel.: 0116 254 9568
Email: enquiries@bps.org.uk
Website: www.bps.org.uk

Australia

Mental Health Foundation of Australia
270 Church Street
Richmond
Victoria 3121
Australia
Tel.: 03 9427 0406
Email: admin@mentalhealthvic.org.au
Website: www.mentalhealthvic.org.au

USA

Mental Health America
2000 North Beauregard Street
6th Floor
Alexandria, VA 22311
USA
Tel.: (703) 684 7722
Toll-free: (800) 969 6642
Website: www.nmha.org

NARSAD: The Mental Health Research Association
60 Cutter Mill Road
Suite 404
Great Neck, NY 11021
USA
Tel.: (800) 829 8289
Email: info@narsad.org
Website: www.narsad.org

National Alliance on Mental Illness
3803 N. Fairfax Drive
Suite 100
Arlington, VA 22201-3042
USA
Tel.: (703) 524 7600
Information helpline: 1-800-950-NAMI (6264)
Website: www.nami.org

National Institute of Mental Health
Public Information and Communications Branch
6001 Executive Boulevard
Room 8184, MSC 9663
Bethesda, MD 20892-9663
USA
Tel.: (301) 443 4513
Toll-free: 1-866-615-6464
Email: nimhinfo@nih.gov
Website: www.nimh.nih.gov

National Mental Health Consumers' Self-Help Clearinghouse
1211 Chestnut Street
Suite 1207
Philadelphia, PA 19107
USA
Tel.: (212) 751 1810
Email: info@mhselfhelp.org
Website: www.mhselfhelp.org

Index

NB: page numbers in italic indicate figures or tables